The Color of Winter

Steelhead Fly Fishing
on the Olympic Peninsula

Doug Rose

Dedication

This book is dedicated to my parents,
Richard and Anna Marie Rose:
They taught me to fish and bought me books.

"It's nearly sixty years since I caught those fish, and steelhead, especially the big winter steelhead, still fascinate me. They bring some of the mysteries from the vast deep with them when they come back to the river."

Syd Glasso, 1970
from The Creel, The Flyfishers Club of Oregon

Cover Photo: Optimist on Hoh River Rocks—Photo and fly by John McMillan.

Acknowledgments

Many people who love wild fish were extremely generous with their time, stories and ideas when I was writing this book, and they had a profound impact on its ultimate shape and content. I would like to express my heartfelt gratitude to all of them. Specifically, I would like to thank Dick Goin, the Olympic Peninsula's great storehouse of angling and salmon lore; Jim Lichatowich, the most eloquent and insightful biologist of his generation; and Buck Adamire, whose delightful letters were a wealth of information on logging, salmon and wildlife. Many biologists were a great help: Mike McHenry, Lower Elwha S'Klallam Tribe; John Meyer, Olympic National Park; John McMillan, Wild Salmon Center; Jill Silver, Hoh Tribe; Peter Bahls, independent fisheries biologist. The West End's great flyfishing guides, Dave Steinbaugh, J.D. Love, Herb Jacobsen, Steve Reed, and Bob Pigott have a lot to do with whatever I know about winter steelhead fly-fishing. Ramon Vanden Brulle and Kurt Beardslee of Washington Trout provided technical literature, and we spent a great day on the Hoh. Jim Kerr and Joe Crecca of the Port Townsend Angler, and, again, Dave Steinbaugh of Waters West Fly Fishing Outfitters were important sources of advice and information. I am also indebted to Jack Datisman for his wonderful painting, and Jay Brevik for his friendship and drift-boat handling. John McMillan deserves additional thanks for his photos, flies and his passion. Like all Northwest steelheaders, I am beholden to Bill McMillan for leading the way for the last thirty years. I would also like to express my deep appreciation to Tom Jay; Tim McNulty, Ron Hirschi, and especially, Jerry Gorsline, whose unswerving dedication to the Olympic Peninsula's natural systems are an inspiration. Finally, thanks to Ellie, Max and Lily for tolerating the combination of contemplation and chaos that I seem to require on a big project.

All inquiries should be addressed to:
Frank Amato Publications, Inc.
P.O. Box 82112, Portland, Oregon 97282
503.653.8108 • www.amatobooks.com

All photographs by John McMillan unless otherwise noted.
Book & Cover Design: Michael Henderson
Printed in Hong Kong
Softbound ISBN: 1-57188-303-7 • UPC: 0-81127-00137-8

10 9 8 7 6 5 4 3 2 1

Table of Contents

Chapter One	The Color of Winter	8
Chapter Two	Queets	15
Chapter Three	West End Steelhead	19
Chapter Four	A Room-Temperature IQ	26
Chapter Five	Ghosts	34
Chapter Six	Bogachiel	41
Chapter Seven	Mr. Glasso's Flies	44
Chapter Eight	Deus Ex Machina	50
Chapter Nine	Winter Solstice	57
Chapter Ten	Hoh	65
Chapter Eleven	Industrial-Strength Flies	68
Chapter Twelve	The Creeks	73
Chapter Thirteen	The Big Rod	80
Chapter Fourteen	Sol Duc	86
Chapter Fifteen	dead-drift	89
Chapter Sixteen	The Park	95
Chapter Seventeen	Maximum Sustained Harvest	102
Chapter Eighteen	Quinault	109
Chapter Nineteen	Garrett's Stoneflies and Feather Wings	112
Chapter Twenty	Timber and Fish	118
Chapter Twenty-One	DixwodAchtada	127
Chapter Twenty-Two	Calawah	131
Chapter Twenty-Three	Refugia	134
Chapter Twenty-Four	The Elwha	141
Chapter Twenty-Five	Calypso Orchids	147

Chapter One

The Color of Winter

The West End of the Olympic Peninsula is a big place, with a lot of rivers and during the winter a lot of steelhead return to these rivers. The Quillayute System tributaries, the fabled Sol Duc, Bogachiel, Calawah and Dickey, have hosted in excess of 15,000 fish in recent years, the largest run of wild winter steelhead in the Pacific Northwest. South of the Quillayute, the rainforest rivers, the Hoh and Queets and Quinault, also receive thousands of steelhead in settings of enormous trees, drooping moss, and nearly constant rain. In between the major rivers, rivers whose names are familiar throughout the world of steelhead fly-fishing, a network of more obscure cedar-stained creeks drain into the Strait of Juan de Fuca and the Pacific Ocean. Once the near-exclusive domain of local anglers, all of these rivers have become the winter destinations of anglers from around the world. A recent survey by the Washington Department of Fish and Wildlife (WDFW) indicated that pressure on the West End rivers increased by 50 percent in the 1990s.

Once you get above the boundaries where people can no longer kill wild steelhead, the fishing can still take on an intimate character. It is fairly easy, in fact, to fish for most of a day without running into another angler. I fished the upper portion of one of the peninsula's most popular rivers once a week a few years ago, and I only ran into one other person, and I knew him. More and more steelheaders haunt these rivers, as the steelhead in other regions have faltered and word of the West End spreads. But in the selective fishery portions of these rivers, which are extensive during winter, the anglers you encounter are increasingly other fly-fishers. And if you are the type of Olympic Peninsula resident who has organized their life around fly-fishing to the extent that you regularly have free time during the week, there is a good chance you will know the people you run into.

Take the late-January day a few years ago when my friend, Jay Brevik, and I fished the upper Sol Duc River. The peninsula had had an especially stormy early winter that year. One low-pressure system after another spun storm after storm into the coast. There had been long stretches when the rivers were out of shape, especially for fly-fishing, but we finally hit a patch of cold dry weather, with clear blue days and sharp frosty nights. The tributaries slowed to a trickle, the glaciers froze up, and the water levels dropped like a bucket of paint from a third-story scaffold. For those of us who have lived on the Peninsula long enough to remember, it seemed like a return to earlier winters. It also looked like a perfect time to go fishing.

"It's supposed to freeze hard again tonight," Jay said, when he called me in the afternoon. "Have you heard from anyone what it's like out there?"

"I just talked to Dave," I said.

Dave Steinbaugh is the owner of Water's West Fly Fishing Outfitters in Port Angeles, and he is also a veteran West End fly-fishing guide. He has his fingers on the pulse of winter steelheading on the Peninsula more than anyone I know. "He said the Hoh was still out but that the Bogachiel and Sol Duc were high but clear."

"How about the roads?"

"I don't know. I didn't think to ask."

It's a two-hour drive from the east side of the peninsula, where Jay and I live, to the upper part of the Sol Duc, and nearly three hours to the upper end of the Bogachiel or Hoh. There are notoriously treacherous spots along the route during freezing weather, at Indian Valley and the stretch between Lake Crescent and Bear Creek, where black ice will spin a vehicle into the ditch in a heartbeat. As a result, we tend to be fairly conscientious about the road conditions. I needed to talk to Bob Pigott anyway, another well-known West End fly-fishing guide who lives a couple miles east of Sappho, so I told Jay I would give him a call.

"How are the roads?" I asked, after we had chatted for a few minutes.

"They're fine in Forks," he said. "But there's about a foot of snow here."

"Are there any fish around?"

"They're getting a few," Bob said. "There aren't many hatchery fish left, though."

I hung up and called Jay back. He had just gotten off the phone with Joe Crecca, who along with Jim Kerr, runs the Port Townsend Angler, Port Townsend's fly shop.

"Yeah," Jay said. "Joe said the same thing about the upper Sol Duc. He said they have been doing good on right-angle nymphing."

"We should go," I said.

Jay picked me up at five a.m. It was cold and clear as we headed west, and it was still dark when we stopped in P.A., as Port Angeles is known on the peninsula, and picked up the flies that Dave had stashed for us outside his shop. We didn't run into any snow until we climbed the Fairholm Hill west of Lake Crescent. Then we could see the luminous white shimmer on the pre-dawn shapes of the fir trees. The tires on Jay's big diesel began to thump on compact ice and snow, rather than the whir they make when driving on dry pavement.

It was about a half-hour after first light when we parked at the end of a two track above the Sol Duc. We could see our breath when we got out of the truck, not a common occurrence on the Olympic Peninsula, even during winter. The snow came to just below my knees. We wriggled into our waders quickly, then strung our rods. It is only about a quarter mile from the end of the road to the section of river we planned to fish, but the trail that once wound through the second-growth hemlock and Douglas fir was obliterated by blowdown years ago. You can't walk more than twenty feet in a straight line in any direction without scrambling over or under a log. It is always hard work, and when you added more than a foot of snow to the equation, it made for slow, laborious going.

Jay is younger than I am and earns his living pulling halibut from Alaskan waters, and is in better shape. He was already standing on the gravel bar staring into a fly box when I reached the high bank above the river. The Sol Duc was in perfect condition—high but with that back-lit shade of emerald that steelheaders call "color." Holding my rod with one hand and clutching roots for balance with the other, I backed down the steep slope to the river. Other than Jay's tracks, there was not a blemish on the snow, not even the sign of a river otter or raven. I decided to take advantage of the rare blanket of snow and retrieved my old Nikon from my daypack. Jay steeped into the sand and cobble shallows and began casting.

I took pictures for about fifteen minutes. Then, as I was putting the camera back into its case, I noticed a boat upstream. Not very many people float this section of the Sol Duc. It has a number of chutes and drops and whitewater, and you shouldn't even try to it unless you are quite handy with oars and know the river. It was also a weekday.

"Look," I hollered to Jay.

Jay turned and glanced upstream. "Isn't that J.D?" he said, as the boat drifted closer.

Sure enough, a couple of minutes later, J.D. Love, one of the West End's most experienced steelhead fly-fishing guides, rowed the boat up into the shallows.

"Hi, guys," he said. "How you doing?"

"We just got here," I said.

"Is that you?" Jay said to one of J.D.'s clients.

"Jay?" the angler said, shaking his head.

It turned out that J.D.'s customers were old friends of Jays from Aberdeen.

"How are you guys doing?" I asked.

"We got a couple of fish earlier," J.D. said.

We chatted for a few minutes, then J.D. shoved off and rowed downstream. I stashed my camera bag and tied a pink Articulated Rabbit Strip Leech on my short leader. I waded upstream to a nice run above a creek mouth, where the river narrows slightly and the bottom is broken by small boulders. At this volume of water, it was a little faster than steelhead usually like, but the seam just upstream, between the heavier water of the main current and the shallows, looked like it could hold a fish.

I stripped out six coils of line, backcast, and shot my sink-tip across and downstream. I worked the seam hard for about fifteen minutes. Nothing. Looking downstream, I could see that Jay had fished down to the end of the run, apparently without connecting either. I waded farther upstream, past a wide shallow riffle, to the tailout below a boulder garden. The trees come down to the bank here, and it was hard to get a good angle for a wet-fly swing from shore. I switched to a floating line and fished a nymph with roll casts. Nothing happened there, either.

After a while, Jay and I switched places. We fished for another hour or so without even sensing the ghost of a fish. Then we clambered up the bank and stomped through the snow back to the truck.

"That was a lot of work," I said, wiping sweat from my forehead.

"Well, that's winter steelhead fly-fishing," Jay said. "Where do you want to go now?"

"We could drive down to the Calawah," I said. "It's probably in good shape, too. Or we could go down to the lower Sol Duc, down to the Bark Hole or the Sand Rock Hole."

"They've probably already been hit pretty hard," he said.

I nodded. As I said, a hell of a lot more people fish these rivers than used to.

The thing we actually ended up doing was staying put. It was only about eleven o'clock, but we had been up for a long time and were hungry. We ate our sandwiches leaning against the truck, as the cold from the snow seeped through our wading shoes and neoprenes. After we finished, we followed the path downstream to a section of pocket water. Situated directly above a long shallow rapids, it is full of deep slots and large boulders. Large Douglas fir and western hemlock shade the river, and its surface is broken by the uneven layer of rocks and gravel on the bottom. In other words, it's a really nice piece of steelhead water.

"I took a nice fish just above that big rock," I said, pointing as Jay waded into the river.

I walked downstream a little ways and began working the fan of slick water above a submerged, flat-topped rock. After a while, the casting, mending, swinging rhythms of the wet-fly swing became hypnotic, as they can when you haven't hooked a fish in a while. It probably shouldn't come as much of a surprise, then, that my mind wandered back to the steelhead I had mentioned to Jay. As a post-fifty-year-old, I increasingly have trouble remembering things that happened to me last week, or even earlier in the day, but to the bemusement of my wife, I seem to be able to recall with intensely vivid detail all of the steelhead I have taken on a fly.

That fish was about fourteen pounds, and it was a wild, with flawless nearly transparent adipose and ventral fins. Its back was a deep charcoal, the color of lampblack, shading to a luminous quicksilver above its lateral line and pale white on the soft flesh below. The dark top/light bottom is protective coloration, common to all anadromous salmonids. It allows them to blend with the water when seen by a kingfisher from above and to disappear into the sky when seen from beneath by a sea lion. But the decorative extravagance of steelhead extends far beyond the realm of camouflage. Seen up close, a winter steelhead's flanks reflect silver and blue and rose, like beads of water on a bare winter branch. The double-ought buckshot spots are a vivid indigo, and the luminous white of its belly is both subtle and intense, like the inside of an oyster shell.

"You want to go somewhere else?" Jay asked, interrupting my reverie.

We hiked back to the car and headed towards Forks. The snow disappeared a short distance west of Beaver, as it often does. Then it began to rain. We drove down to the take-out on the Rayonier 3000 Road and looked at the new boat ramp. There was way too much activity on the lower river for fly-fishing, so we backtracked to the South Fork of the Calawah. We fished a few slots and holes downstream of Hyas Creek. By then, it was early afternoon and we were ready to head home. We stopped at the Hungry Bear Cafe and picked up coffee. Then, leaving the little cluster of humanity at Bear Creek, we came out into the open of the big clear-cut by the scaling station. As always, when I drive through this stretch, my gaze was drawn up to the tangle of peaks at the headwaters of the Sol Duc, southeast of the road.

I have carried my old green Kelty pack among those ridges and peaks many times during late summer and autumn, but on this short winter afternoon, they were hidden behind dense charcoal clouds. In the middle distance, the timber-furrowed ridges still wore a mantle of white, obscuring their usual conifer green. The snow was already melting on the clear cut, and it was washed with the flat, pale afternoon light. Connecting it all, falling on the old firs of the upper Sol Duc, the second-growth of Calawah Ridge and the stumps and slash of the clear-cut, was the silver curtain of rain. It occurred to me that the charcoal and oyster and silver that steelhead wear when they return from the sea are also, along with its perennial carpet of green, the essential palette of an Olympic Peninsula winter.

More than any other species of Northwest salmonid, the wild steelhead that return to Olympic Peninsula rivers are the color of winter.

Chapter Two
QUEETS

When Franklin Roosevelt visited the West End of the Olympic Peninsula in 1937, he was appalled by the size and devastation of many of the clear cuts. "I hope the son-of-a-bitch who logged that is roasting in hell," he said, as he passed an especially egregious clear cut south of the Hoh River. Roosevelt subsequently resolved that Olympic National Park should contain one western rainforest valley from the mountains to the sea. After much wrangling with local chambers of commerce and a controversial condemnation of Queets valley homesteads, the Queets Corridor was added to the park in 1953 by Roosevelt's successor, Harry Truman. A mile wide finger of land along the north and south banks of the river, it extended from the original 1938 park boundary to the Quinault Indian Reservation, six miles above the river's mouth on the ocean. The Queets basin is much larger than the area within the national park, of course, and the forests outside the park have been subjected to intensive timber harvest. But the Queets River, nonetheless, enjoys more protection than any other major river on the peninsula.

"It's a good fishery," said Clay Butler, a Quinault Tribe member, long-time Olympic National Park ranger and veteran fly-fishing guide. "The early season for winter steelhead begins before December, right around Thanksgiving. It can be good early up to the Salmon River. What I do is look at the Clearwater. If it's in reasonable shape, I stay on the reservation and guide on the Queets. The fish congregate below the Clearwater. They are pretty receptive to flies unless it gets too dirty. If it's too dirty, I fish the part of the Salmon in the reservation."

The question of whether a river is "in shape" for fly-fishing is one of the most discussed topics on the Olympic Peninsula, and it is talked about more in regard to the Queets than any other river. The region's second-largest system, with a drainage of 445 square miles, the Queets is fed by glaciers on Mount Olympus and the heaviest annual precipitation in the region. A big jade brute of a river, it tends to have both higher average and peak flows than any other West End river. It also has blue clay deposits that bleed into it during heavy rain. As a result, the Queets is in condition for fly-fishing fewer days each winter than any other West End river. "It doesn't have to be raining for the Queets to go out," the late Roy Bergstrom used to say. "It only has to look like rain." During early winter, the best conditions occur when a modest spurt of rain is followed by a sharp cold snap, one that puts black ice on Highway 101.

The "Clearwater" that Clay Butler refers to is the Clearwater River. The Queets' largest tributary, it drains 153 square miles between the Queets and Hoh, an area larger than the Bogachiel watershed, before flowing into the mainstem just upstream of the reservation. Its headwaters on Mount Octopus and Hueldsonk Ridge are too low for glaciers, and it runs much cleaner than the mainstem. When the lower Queets is out, many anglers turn their sights to the Clearwater. The "Salmon" is the next major tributary upstream, and it is the site of the Quinault Tribe's hatchery. In recent years, it has released between 75,000 and 150,000 winter steelhead smolts, as well as coho and chinook. Upstream of Salmon River, wild fish predominate year round, and the major tributaries are Matheny Creek, Sams River and, beyond the end of the road, Tshletshy Creek.

"It gets pounded real heavy from Salmon River down during the early season," said John Meyer, Olympic National Park fisheries biologist. "Then later on when there are more wild fish in the river people move up to the campground."

Wild steelhead return to the Queets every month of the year. As with the other rainforest rivers, however, it also hosts one of the most diverse assortments of migratory salmonids in North America. By mid-February, when the bulk of the wild steelhead run is moving into the upper river, the vanguard of the spring chinook run begins nosing into tidewater. Weighing upwards of 50 pounds, these fish will spawn far above the end of the Queets River Road at the campground, up to Kilkelly Rapids. Andromous char, both Dolly Varden and bull trout, swim in the opposite direction a few weeks later, heading for rich saltwater feeding grounds.

Sea-run cutthroat also drop down to saltwater in spring, about the same time that the first summer steelhead return to the river. Summer and fall chinook, coho and small numbers of chum salmon appear in staggered pulses until the first early-timed winter steelhead nose up into the river with the first late fall tides and rain.

The fact that the Queets flows entirely through a national park and Indian reservation has not made it immune to problems. Indeed, the 13 miles of gravel road along the south bank of the river between Highway 101 and the Queets Campground contains three boat launches. Since the National Park liberalized bait-angling regulations and raised the limit on wild harvest in the late 1990s, there has been a corresponding increase in harassment of fly-fishers on and off the river, as well as some vandalism of vehicles. The fish aren't doing that well, either. From the early 1990s, when the Queets was one of the few major Northwest rivers with an increasing wild-run size, the numbers fell off dramatically in the mid and late 1990s. Mandatory wild release regulations and bait prohibitions were implemented in March of 2001; the same emergency regulations were imposed in 2002 and the season closed entirely on March, rather than on the traditional April 15 closer.

"It was an abomination," said J.D. Love, who has a permit to guide in the national park. "There was a lot of illegal harvest. The restrictions made a big difference in the crowds. It was a good first step. But the park has a reputation for lax enforcement. Frankly, I would like to see boats for transportation only on the Queets. One of the more popular techniques there is side drifting with roe. They get 15 or 20 fish a day. That's not fishing with a conscience. Less boat traffic would make a higher quality of fishery. That would give every fisherman in the park equal access. If there is a parade of boats it is not really very enjoyable."

Despite the problems, the Queets is still more of a steelhead system than most rivers are in their prime, and an intrepid fly-fisher can discover superb fishing and solitude. There are miles of water between the boat launches, and an angler willing to bushwhack the half-mile or so to the river from the road can enjoy first water long before the boats have a chance to reach it. A hiker willing to camp, willing to pack in a seam-sealed tent, a sleeping bag, a stove and a couple of freeze dried meals, can fish last light and first light undisturbed. A boat provides access to even more pristine water, because you can paddle over to the Queets River Trail, which is located on the opposite side of the river from the campground. Nearly always inaccessible during high flows, the trail is virtually deserted during the winter. Prominently displayed NRA and Rush Limbaugh bumperstickers are good insurance for your vehicle.

"J.D. and I fished the upper river on the last day of the season last year," said Dave Steinbaugh. "We fished it hard all day. Late in the day we waded the river. It was that low. It was probably lower then than it was in September. I caught a real nice fish. It hit a purple and peacock fly about four inches long."

Chapter Three

West End Steelhead

It is pretty easy to devolve into a litany of superlatives when writing about the Olympic Peninsula. It has the *tallest* trees. It receives the *most* rain. It has the *highest* mountains in the coast range. It has the lowest-elevation glacier complexes south of Alaska. It was one of the *first* places seen by European sea captains. British Captain John Meares named the tallest snow-capped peak he observed in the region Mount Olympus in 1788, after the home of the gods in Greek mythology. Yet even the lowest pass in the Olympic Mountains wasn't successfully traversed by Euro-Americans until 1890. A century later, the Olympic Peninsula still has more wild country, including nearly 900,000 acres in Olympic National Park, than any other region in the Northwest. You are as likely to see an elk as a Holstein on the Upper Hoh Road on a winter morning, and if you live on the West End, your children will be deprived of network television unless you are willing to pony up for a satellite dish.

There is one other area where the West End of the Olympic Peninsula surpasses every other region of the Pacific Northwest: It grows more wild winter steelhead. There are bigger rivers, and there are rivers where anglers harvest more fish, and there are rivers that have a longer history of fly-fishing, but there is no place in the world with either the abundance of fish or the diversity of opportunity as the rivers that drain the West End of the Olympic Peninsula. Indeed, 10 out of 15 of the National Marine Fisheries Service's (NFMS) Evolutionarily Significant Units (ESU) of steelhead are currently protected under the Endangered Species Act, and the Oregon Coast and Klamath Mountain Province populations only escaped listing after the states agreed to significantly modify hatchery and harvest practices. The wild winter steelhead of Puget Sound and eastern Olympic Peninsula rivers have, moreover, virtually collapsed since NFMS reviewed their status. Only the wild steelhead native to the remote and rainy West End of the Olympic Peninsula remain worthy of the description "healthy."

"I guess I am probably here because of the steelhead fishing," J.D. Love told me when I asked him why he lived on the West End. As a fly-fishing guide he has extensive experience in Montana, Alaska and the Grande Ronde, and he could set up a shingle anyplace he wanted. "I grew up steelhead fishing. I caught my first on the Quinault River. I would have stayed in Montana if trout were my main interest. And I seriously considered southeast Alaska. I've spent bits and pieces of 10 years there. But there are no big rivers on those islands. There are good runs but there isn't the variety. I also like the marine environment of the Olympic Peninsula and the seafood. But basically I just love to fly-fish for steelhead."

The appellation "West End," incidentally, is as much a concept as it is a geographic description. It usually refers to the area west of Lake Crescent and north of Lake Quinualt, a roughly 50-by-60-mile triangle of trees and rivers. Perhaps not entirely coincidentally, that area corresponds roughly with the boundaries of NMFS's Olympic Peninsula ESU. Reduced to its most basic, the fish within an ESU have more in common with each other, genetically and in life history patterns, than they do with fish from outside their native range. One of the ways that Olympic Peninsula winter steelhead are different is that they are older when they return to fresh water than most winter steelhead. That expresses itself in big fish. Winter steelhead in excess of 30 pounds are taken every year on these rivers, and during the early 1980s the Quinault Tribe netted a 37-pound fish.

"There weren't many steelhead in the Lyre," said Dick Goin, a Port Angeles angler who has fished the Olympic Peninsula streams for 60 years. "but they were the ugliest, meanest steelhead on the Peninsula. I fished the Thompson River a few years ago and this guy said, 'You'll be lucky if you don't get cleaned once a year on these fish.' I said, 'That's nice but I fish the Olympic Peninsula and I used to get cleaned out every three fish.' I think they were so fierce because the temperature was higher and they adapted to the steep gradient. They had long huge tails. Those fish had one method of fighting. They just started jumping and headed down river."

With more than two dozen rivers open during the winter and a season that is nearly six months long, the West End has gradually emerged, as Yellowstone and the Everglades did before it, as one of those truly rare places where the fly-fishing diversity and abundance possess a mythic richness and intensity. Within the Quillayute System itself, the Calawah flows clearly and deliberately over broken shelves and boulders, while the nearby Sol Duc bubbles over elaborate rock gardens, and the Bogachiel sidles around gravel bars and dark sentinels of spruce. A twenty-minute drive over Burnt Mountain from the Sol Duc, the Pysht River is tanin-stained, brushy and scarcely a cast wide, yet it has turned out 20-pound steelhead. To the south, the glacial rainforest rivers are the wildest of all, where wilderness is within reach of a short winter hike and where steelhead enter the river every month of the year.

Depending upon whom you talk to, temperate zone rain forests can be found from Northern California to southeast Alaska, even east in northwest Montana by some reckonings. On the Olympic Peninsula, however, people are a little more fussy about the term and reserve it for the Hoh, Queets and Quinault valleys. For one thing, these southwest-oriented, ocean-facing valleys receive even more rain than the Bogachiel River valley to the north or the Humptulips to the south. They also have larger trees—including the largest Douglas fir, western hemlock and western redcedar in the world—and the heaviest canopies of moss in the Northwest. Unlike the Quillayute System and creeks, the rainforest rivers are also fed by glaciers. A number of Northwest rivers, some of them considerably larger than West End rivers, are also glacial systems, but the Hoh, Queets and Quinault are the only glacial rivers on the West Coast south of Alaska that flow directly into the Pacific Ocean. This combination of coastal rain forest and glaciers has created river systems that are, by even the most literal interpretation of the word, unique.

In terms of just plain-old bigness, however, nothing approaches the Quillayute System. "I doubt if many people are aware of just how immense this drainage really is," Buck Adamire wrote me a few years ago. An avid outdoorsman, Buck logged on the West End for nearly 50 years, and he hunted, fished and trapped nearly every inch of the Quillayute. "If you examine a map of the entire county, this river drains very close to one third of Clallam County and small portions of Jefferson. Even though the Quillayute drains a huge area, the amount of water exiting in the ocean during summer is low due to the fact that none of the tributaries are fed by glacier melt. The actual water feeding the system varies in that some originates from muskeg-like cedar swamp meadows; crystal-clear springs along the Calawah, Sol Duc, Bogachiel and Dickey rivers, as well as snow melt and, of course, ordinary rain."

Then there are the creeks. John Meyer is the head fisheries biologist at Olympic National Park. During his 16 years at Olympic, as it is known on the Peninsula, he has snorkeled its large rivers and its small, including some of the remote creeks that flow through its coastal strip. "I was snorkeling it in June one year," he said, talking about a small creek that flows into the Pacific Ocean miles from the nearest road. "There is not a lot of spawning habitat, but the steelhead were using it very heavily. I saw substantial numbers of steelhead redds. I have never seen that density of redds. They were everywhere where gravel occurred."

Perhaps the best way to understand why West End steelhead have prevailed while other stocks of *mykiss*, including neighboring Olympic Peninsula stocks, have fallen on hard times is to look at a map. The most obvious thing about the Quillayute System, rainforest rivers and cedar creeks is that they are a long way from just about everywhere. This isolation has served as a buffer against civilization, especially the habitat conversion that has installed trophy homes, dairy farms, mines, reservoirs, alfalfa fields and, in many instances, towns and cities in steelhead habitat. There is a long history of logging in the region. It has done grievous harm to salmonid habitat in the past, and there are also continuing abuses, but West End steelhead have recovered from cyclical flooding, fire, hurricane force winds and droughts for centuries, and they have also demonstrated the capacity to endure a certain level of timber harvest.

If you look more closely at the same map, you will also notice that a huge area, roughly one-fourth of its land mass, more than 1,600 square miles, lies within Olympic National Park. "In less than 80 years some of the world's most productive temperate rainforest was converted to tree farms," Michael McHenry, James Lichatowich and Rachel Kowalski-Hagamman observed in their

1996 report, "Status of Salmon and Their Habitats on the Olympic Peninsula, Washington." "A diverse network of large and small streams flowed through those old-growth forests and supported abundant population of Pacific salmon. Parts of those streams, primarily the upper portions of the largest systems (Soleduck, Bogachiel, Hoh and Queets rivers) were ultimately included in the boundaries of Olympic National Park. Those areas are now refugia for some species, particularly steelhead and Chinook salmon."

A final, even closer look at the map reveals that the rivers flow outward from the vaguely concentric core of the Olympic Mountains in a radial pattern. Some rivers run north to the Strait of Juan de Fuca, others drain east into Hood Canal or south into the Chehalis River, and still others run west, to the Pacific Ocean. Because each valley faces the prevailing southwesterly weather systems from a slightly different aspect, Olympic Peninsula rivers exhibit a dramatic range of climatic variation. The rivers that drain the leeward "rain shadow" of the northeastern Olympics receive less than 20 inches of rain annually. On the opposite side of the mountains, the valleys of the Hoh and Queets and Quinault rivers absorb the heaviest precipitation in the lower 48 states, around 90 inches in the lowlands and more than 200 on the slopes of Mount Olympus. In between these extremes, each Olympic Peninsula watershed has adapted to its rainfall, drainage pattern and topography.

The intriguing thing about this distribution of weather and rivers is that it replicates to a remarkably accurate degree the conditions encountered by winter steelhead throughout the Washington, Oregon and California. The Dungeness River and the small streams that drain the Olympic rainshadow flow through terrain similar to Southern Oregon and Northern California, even to the point of containing prickly pear cactus and juniper. Although their downward pitches from the high country are shorter than Puget Sound streams, the glacially-influenced Dosewallips and Duckabush rivers are similar in many ways to the Nisqually and Puyallup rivers. The rainfall is heavier on the south flank of the Olympics, and anglers from the Siletz or Alsea will recognize the streamers of moss and the salal thickets on the Wynoochee and Satsop.

Only the rivers of the West End of the Olympic Peninsula have no ecosystem counterparts anywhere. This is partly the function of the forests and partly the glaciers, but the underlying factor that connects everything on the West End is the rain. It arrives in a multitude of forms—in squalls and torrential downpours, as drizzle and sleet, and as mist and snow and saturating fog. Nearly all of the 200 inches of precipitation on Mount Olympus and the Bailey Range, which are located only about 50 miles from the breakers of the Pacific Ocean, falls as snow. That is like 200 inches of snow falling on Olympia or Portland or Eugene. Even during summer, when rainfall all but ceases on the West End, the condensation from the oceanic fog that drifts up river valleys accounts for approximately 35 inches of precipitation a year. That's more rain than falls in Sequim in two years. From fog drip!

All of this rain has to go somewhere, and the majority of it is ferried out to sea in rivers. That means they are unfishable a fair amount of the time during winter, sometimes for a week on the glacial rivers. This allows many steelhead to escape fishermen, even tribal fishers, when the water is high enough. In addition to providing cover for fish, the rain maintains and creates habitat. High flows carve into stream banks, uprooting the trees and mining the gravel for log jams and spawning beds. The heavy flows that the winter steelhead of West End rivers must negotiate, moreover, and the dynamic, shifting nature of the river channels may also select for the large, strong "nasty" steelhead of which Dick Goin spoke.

"You see the biggest steelhead redds in the lower 48 states on these rivers," said John McMillan, a former fisheries biologist with the Hoh Tribe and currently the Olympic Peninsula representative of the Wild Salmon Center. "It's not uncommon for the fish to move rocks up to 12 inches in diameter. On these short, steep rivers, maybe the migrating females need to be big enough to dig redds that escape scour."

The fact that Olympic Peninsula steelhead are not currently in danger of extinction does not mean that they are anywhere near their historic population levels. No one really knows how many steelhead returned to the Hoh or the Calawah, the Queets or the Sol Duc when Vancouver first saw Mount Olympus, but there are far fewer wild steelhead on many small streams today than there were 20 years ago, and considerably less return to the large systems than when Dick Goin began fishing more than a half century ago. There has also been measurable gene flow between hatchery steelhead and wild fish in some populations, especially the smaller rivers. The Washington Department Fish and Wildlife continues to encourage anglers to kill wild steelhead on 13 West End rivers, and the Washington Fish and Wildlife Commission seems determined to finish off once and for all the remnants of the wild early-timed winter steelhead.

Perfidy aside, if you want to cast a fly for a wild winter steelhead, there is still no better place between late November and the end of April than the West End of the Olympic Peninsula. Indeed, steelhead from these rivers routinely demonstrate the absurdity of the term "winter" steelhead. "The earliest winter steelhead I've caught was in early October on the Quillayute," J.D. Love told me. "It was 39 inches long." At the other end of the continuum, John McMillan recently caught a large unspawned Sol Duc hen in late June. "Its anus was extended but hadn't spawned yet," he said.

"It has a good May run," Dick Goin said of a small stream he has fished for decades. "It has a big pulse of late fish. I would run into them when I was counting redds. Last year, I saw a whole school of big bright fish, beautiful white buggers. That day I saw 33 visuals."

As Mike McHenry, a veteran habitat biologist with the Elwha S'Klallam Tribe told me a number of years ago when we talked about efforts to impose wild release regulations for steelhead on West End rivers:

"They're sitting on a gold mine out there."

Chapter Four

A Room-Temperature IQ

Any day that I hook a winter steelhead with a fly is a rip-roaring skyrocket of a success as far as I am concerned. It doesn't really matter if I land the fish or not. When I fish the streams of the Olympic Peninsula's West End, my goal is to hook one fish a day. Meager as that ambition may seem, it is one I only achieve on a fitful and sometimes infuriating basis. Dave Steinbaugh manages considerably better. He expects to catch a winter steelhead every time he fishes. So does J. D. Love. Former fly-fishing guides Herb Jacobsen and Bob Pigott did, as well. During one season in the early 1990s, Bob managed to connect his clients, who presumably possessed widely varying levels of ability, with 140 winter steelhead.

For me, though, the fish usually come a lot farther apart. I went the entire winter without a steelhead when I first began to fish out here, and I repeated the process a few years ago when I was learning to fish with my Spey rod. I'm not the only one who experiences these occasional droughts, either, and some are very good fly-fishers. "I average 30 winter steelhead a year on the fly," John McMillan told me recently. "But I fished 45 days without a fish last year."

That's why I remember the day I hooked two steelhead within a half hour. I was on the upper Hoh, above the last upstream boat ramp. It was early winter, the wettest time of year on the West End, but we had enjoyed a mild early winter, almost an extension of autumn. The river was low, low enough that I could actually wade the head of a shallow riffle above my favorite pool. It is one of my most dependable holes, one that I have taken not only steelhead from, but also chinook, coho, cutthroat, anadromous char and whitefish. The Hoh was as clear as it gets in winter, but it still carried the shimmering green the helps mask a fly line.

I had an entirely new perspective from the south bank. Instead of dropping off quickly into deep water, this side of the river tapered gradually into the main channel. I had always fished the top of the pool with a floating line and long leader before. It was impossible to work with a wet-fly swing from the north bank, because it was too deep to wade and drooping alder branches made the casting angle from shore impossible. The broad, gravelly tailout was always more inviting at high water, anyway. But at this water level the frothy boulders at the head of the pool looked much more promising, and the south side of the river was a perfect place to set up a wet-fly swing.

There are several seemingly conflicting conventional wisdoms regarding fly selection out here. One maintains that you fish darker patterns early in the run and brighter ones later. I have also heard that larger flies work best on fresh fish in the lower river, while smaller ones are best upstream. I tend to ignore the prescriptions and stick with patterns that have caught me fish in the past. So I chose a mahogany and black Marabou Spider. My line was a 15-foot Type III sink-tip. I took up position about a third of the way across the river. Even at low water, I could feel the Hoh digging at the gravel beneath my wading shoes.

I began with short casts. I fished the area below me on tight swings, with only about twenty feet of line. Then, staying in the same place, I began to extend my casts. I began to place the fly closer and closer to the deep water. I tossed a mend each time, to straighten the line, then followed it with the rod as it worked its way down and then across stream. I was trying to lead the fly slowly across the upstream face of the soft water. I was a little rusty, not having fished for a couple of weeks, and it took a while to determine the best angle for the cast but I finally maneuvered the line where I wanted it, along the edge of the boulders. I swung it back along the seam between the broken water at the head of the pool and the softer water downstream.

The fly had ticked about halfway back to the bank when I felt the fish. There was a brief bump, followed by an almost weightless feeling. I struck with the rod and my line hand. Suddenly, there was that thrilling head shake. The steelhead broke the surface, not jumping as they usually do, but wallowing, like a chinook in salt water. I leaned back on the rod a second time, to make sure the hook was set. It shook its head again and streaked downstream, then jumped, a low somersaulting leap. It was a thick-bodied fish of about 12 or 14 pounds. Its dull pewter flanks carried a ribbon of rose. It landed on the leader, neatly severing the line.

"Damn it," I said.

This is probably the most famous sentence written about steelhead fly-fishing in the last twenty years: "The biggest things a steelheader or Atlantic salmon fisherman can have—not counting waders and a stipend—are a big arm and a room-temperature IQ."

Thomas McGuane wrote the line, and it appeared in *Harper's Magazine* in 1984. McGuane is the author of many novels and essay collections, including *Ninety-Two in the Shade* and *To Skin a Cat*. He also writes regularly about fly-fishing. If the number of McGuane citations in recent books and essays on fly fishing is any indication, he is the favorite writer of virtually every middle-aged white male former English major who owns a fly rod. His line about steelhead, of course, refers to the wet-fly swing, the traditional fly-fishing presentation for steelhead, especially winter steelhead. Among many fly-fishers who fish dry flies or nymphs on drag-free floats for resident trout, the wet-fly swing is seen as a rather primitive form of fly-fishing,

Actually, I think McGuane was joking. He has written about steelhead fly-fishing with affection and has even fished the West End rivers during winter. I don't know what sort of presentation he used when he was here, but the majority of Olympic Peninsula winter steelhead are taken on the wet-fly swing. As I did that morning on the Hoh, the line is cast down and across stream and swung slowly across the grain of the current. This certainly doesn't require the finesse of, say, feathering a number 22 Tricorythodes two feet above a brown trout on Armstrong's Spring Creek. But the wet-fly swing isn't exactly the fly-fishing equivalent of soaking Velveeta and WD40 in old fishnet stockings for channel catfish, either. Moreover, on the West End rivers its rhythm and deliberation mesh perfectly with the slower metabolism of winter fish.

"I prefer to swing flies," J.D. Love told me, as we spoke one autumn day in his riverside fly-tying cabin. "Some people are busy people. They tend to like methods that demand a lot of attention to detail. Swinging flies is a lot more relaxed method of fishing. I have always figured it is the classic way to steelhead. It's a relaxed and almost meditative way of fishing. I also like having something to look at."

The wet-fly swing is probably the original way flies were presented to fish by human beings. It took Atlantic salmon in Scotland, brown trout in England, and brook trout in New England long before anyone had ever heard of a steelhead. On the West Coast, it was used as a steelhead technique on the Eel River before the turn of the 19th century. For Olympic Peninsula anglers, however, the closest early application of the wet-fly swing for winter steelhead occurred, as did so many of the traditions of winter steelheading, on nearby Vancouver Island. General Noel Money, the retired British brigadier who introduced two-handed rods and Atlantic salmon techniques to British Columbia, caught winter steelhead on flies in the Stamp and Coquihalla rivers as early as the 1920s. Money is also credited with introducing the fly rod as a winter steelheading tool to Roderick Haig-Brown, who had taken all of his previous winter fish on an artificial lure, the Devon Minnow.

"In the original edition of *The Western Angler* I said that it is not easy to catch winter steelhead on the fly," Haig-Brown wrote in the 1947 edition of the book. "I have now completely changed that opinion. During the winter of 1938-1939 I began to use the fly at least as frequently as the minnow and found myself doing not too badly with it. Since then I have used the fly exclusively and, as nearly as I can judge, its effectiveness is at least seventy percent that of the minnow. As time goes on I catch more and more fish on the fly in water that was unfishable or that seemed unproductive with the minnow; and I am inclined to believe that if I can continue to improve my techniques and my knowledge of the river I may find that the fly catches me just as many fish as the minnow ever did."

The basic wet-fly swing is fairly straightforward: You cast across and downstream. A large mend is tossed upstream. The rod tip is held high while the slack of the mend allows the fly to sink and the line to straighten out downstream. When you feel the line begin to pulse against the current, lower the rod and lead the line across the current. The goal is to move the fly slowly, slightly more slowly than the current speed, and at a depth it will be seen by a steelhead. The variations of presentation are endless, because each piece of water requires you to estimate the current speed and depth in order to determine how far upstream you lead your cast. The type of fly also has a bearing on the angle of the cast, with lighter hooks and flies necessitating a fatter angle and heavy flies letting you work a tighter swing. The type of line, obviously, also has a major effect on how deeply and how quickly the fly will sink.

"For winter, I try to work my fly really slowly, to sort of hang the fly," Dave Steinbaugh said. "I just try to move it really slowly. I want it hanging as much as swinging. You can't avoid having it sink. One of the keys with sink-tips is that it is very important to first mend the line to keep it in a straight line."

On paper this may not sound very complicated, and the wet-fly swing is indeed the first technique many beginning fly-fishers are taught, but a lot of accomplished trout fly-fishers apparently underestimate the skill necessary to set up a good wet-fly swing. "What I've discovered is that most people don't have the ability to fish well enough for these fish," fly-fishing guide Herb Jacobsen told me a few years ago. "They don't cast well enough or handle line well enough. Most can't cast beyond 50 feet and most don't know how to mend properly. I usually spend two-thirds of the day teaching people. Most of being successful with these fish is presentation."

Unlike in traditional trout fly-fishing, the line has as much to do with success in winter steelheading as the fly. And, boy, have they come a long way since Syd Glasso coated his lines with red lead in the 1950s. Renowned West End wildlife artist Jack Datisman told me recently that Glasso's protégé, Dick Wentworth, still fishes home-made shooting heads. And Dick Goin and John McMillan fish floating lines exclusively. Manufactured sink-tips, which basically consist of a sinking portion of fly line bonded to a floating running line, are by far the most commonly used lines on the Quillayute System and rainforest rivers today. Developed in the late 1960s, the early sink-tips didn't handle particularly well and their lengths and sinking densities were more appropriate for trout than winter steelhead, but their potential was obvious, and the introduction of Jim Teeny's T-series of 24-foot sink-tips in the 1970s revolutionized winter steelhead fly-fishing.

Today, there are two broad categories of sink-tips—long tips and short tips. The short tips usually have sinking portions from around 5 feet to about 15 feet, while the longer tips are usually from 17 feet to 24 feet, or even longer. As a rule, the shorter tips sink slightly more slowly, and the floating portion handles more like traditional floating lines. They are classified by their manufacturers with Roman or Arabic numerals that indicate their sink rate. For steelhead, Type III (or Type 3) through Type VI (Type 6) are the most popular, and they sink at roughly the speed in seconds of their number designation—that is, a Type III line will sink at about three inches per second. The longer tips sink faster and deeper and usually shoot farther. Taking the lead from the Teeny lines, they are usually identified by their weight in grains.

"I mostly use a Type VI for the Sol Duc," Dave Steinbaugh said. "I use a heavier line on the Sol Duc than the Bogachiel or the Hoh. I like a 150- to 200-grain line for the flatter, broader runs and wider swings on the Hoh. I tend to like a little heavier tip. If the water is shallow, I'll change my angle or use a lighter wire hook. I prefer the 12- to 15-foot sink-tips, and rarely use the 24-foot tips. They can be effective on the large, wide, deep holes, though. The 5-foot tips also have an application if they are heavy enough to swing and hang flies. They might be good on the Hoko or Sekiu."

Of course, the variety of water types on the peninsula make it difficult for one sink-tip to perform optimally under all situations, even on the same river. "Ideally, we'll have rods with Teeny 300 and 500 and Scientific Anglers Type V 13-foot sink-tips rigged up in the boat," Bob Pigott told me a few years ago. It's hard to drag around a handful of rods when you are fishing by yourself, though. Until a few years ago, spare spools were the answer, but they weren't without their own drawbacks. For one, they required you to respool your rod when you wanted to change lines, often with wet hands while wading or standing in a boat. Steelhead quality spools aren't inexpensive, either. The recent introduction of multi-tip lines by the Rio Company, and their subsequent adoption by all the major line manufacturers has been a significant boon to winter steelheaders.

"The multi-tip lines are great," Dave Steinbaugh said. "I love them, although I like my loops better."

And my second steelhead that morning? Well, I hooked it on a wet-fly swing, as well, although not while the fly was actually swinging. After losing the first fish, I stripped in my line and waded back to shore. There really wasn't anyplace else to fish from that side of the river, so I decided to rest the hole. None of my friends can stand this sort of thing—walking an hour or more to fish a drift the size of an Airstream trailer. But I figure that if I don't catch a steelhead every trip anyway, then why shouldn't I fish in a beautiful place where I don't have to look at anyone? I replaced the last foot of my 12-pound test, five-foot leader and tied on another spider. I found my ham sandwich and orange in my day pack. I killed about 20 minutes eating, daydreaming and watching a water ouzel cull next year's stonefly crop. Then I resumed my position at the head of the pool.

I stripped a few loops of line and cast. I intentionally cast farther downstream than I had so far that morning. My leader unfolded five or six feet into the wavy water below the rocks. I threw a big mend, then concentrated on the tip of the floating portion of my line. In the fast water, it didn't take long before it was hanging directly downstream. I stripped a foot or so of line. Then, just as I was about to retrieve the remainder and cast again, I remembered a passage from Roderick Haig-Brown.

"I prefer if possible to be wading almost directly upstream of such a place," he had written in *The Western Angler*, "so that I can hang the fly there as long as possible, fishing it back and forth across the lie by the swing of my rod, drawing it back to me sometimes and letting it drift down again. It may be that many of the fish that take hold in such places have followed the fly around. But I have several times hooked fish after hanging my fly for a full minute or more."

I did exactly as Haig-Brown suggested, letting the fly swing around in the frothy water. The steelhead hit it hard and going away. It hooked itself, and when I hauled back on the rod it exploded in an end over end leap. Then, rather than swim downstream, it scorched towards me. Reeling desperately to gather the slack line, I thought that it would toss the fly any minute. It came within 10 feet, but then bore back downstream. By now, I had it on the reel. I followed it through the sandy shallows. Presently, I managed to turn it and lead it to shore, but it immediately broke for deeper water. But five minutes later I eased it up onto my palm.

It couldn't have been much different from the first fish—only about five pounds and as bright as a bead of mercury. It was a wild fish, one of the small wild fish you often encounter during the early season. I eased the hook from its mouth and released it.

Chapter Five
Ghosts

A few years ago, I drove up to Jim Lichatowich's house in the upper Dungeness River valley on a stormy late-fall afternoon. We had arranged to discuss Jim's book, *Salmon Without Rivers*, which had just been released to widespread acclaim. An internationally-respected fisheries biologist, researcher and eloquent wild-salmonid advocate, Jim was one of the biologists who first raised the alarm about the grave state of Pacific salmon in the 1993 report, "Salmon at the Crossroads." The former number-two man with the Oregon Department of Fish and Wildlife fish division, Jim had abandoned upper-level management a few years earlier and returned to the watersheds as a consulting biologist. We talked about a wide range of topics that afternoon, but one of the concepts that Jim repeatedly returned to was the importance of the diverse life histories that salmon and steelhead had evolved in the Pacific Northwest.

"One of the legacies of the salmon historically in the Northwest is their diverse life histories," he said at one point. "That's a legacy of a region that is so geologically active. In the Rogue River we now see eight or nine different life histories for chinook salmon. But in pristine Russian rivers they are seeing 17 or 18 life histories. These complex sets of life history pathways were their insurance policies when they encountered drought or poor ocean conditions. What has happened here is habitat destruction and some management policies have eliminated a lot of life histories. Now a lot of rivers only have one or two life histories. If we are going to restore healthy runs of salmon, we need to restore these ghosts."

One of the Olympic Peninsula life histories that is well on its way to becoming a ghost is its early run of wild winter steelhead. Historically, the steelhead that entered fresh water during November, December and January comprised a significant, perhaps dominant, component of the winter run. In a report to the Washington Fish and Wildlife Commission (Commission) in support of wild release regulations during the early season, former Kaufmann's Streamborn employee Brian McLachlin submitted net harvest reports prior to 1960 and sport figures from the 1950s that suggested the early-timed component of wild winter steelhead on the Quillayute System rivers was approximately 35 percent of the total run. McLachlin buttressed his facts with even more compelling evidence: The Quileute Indian name for the month we call December translates as "time of the first spawning of steelhead salmon;" their name for January was "peak of steelhead spawning."

Like many veteran Olympic Peninsula anglers, Dick Goin has been intimately acquainted with the early run of wild winter steelhead. "My fishing partner and I got in on the ground floor of buying surplus Army inflatable rafts in 1949 or 1950," he told me. "We used to toss one in at the mouth of the South Fork of the Sol Duc and float down to Hucklesville. That was a little settlement." This is in the upper Sol Duc, above the upper limit of winter steelhead fishing today and adjacent to Olympic National Park. "Here's the significant thing," Dick continued. "The winter steelhead season opened on the first Sunday of December back then. Our preferred thing was to open the season there. We knew there would be a good number of fish. Some already had pink plates. They were big, too. It's hard to remember any under 10 pounds and there were a lot of 12- to 16-pound fish. We got into bigger ones, too, but didn't usually get any of the big honkers in. But we always quit fishing the upper river by February 15. There were too many kelts by then, and those days we used to avoid the kelts like the plague."

Goin says that all of the major West End rivers had significant early runs of winter steelhead in the 1940s, 50s and 60s. "I used to fish the streams that flow into the Strait of Juan de Fuca in the forties. Those rivers all had early runs. They had good-sized runs in November and by the first Sunday in December some of the fish already had rose-colored gill plates. When they planted Chambers Creek fish, they wiped out the early runs."

I fish all of the rivers that Dick talks about. Like him, I have especially strong ties with the Sol Duc, the Hoh, and the rivers that drain into the strait. And I still take large, early wild fish from time to time. But not many. Nor has anyone else in recent years. There simply aren't very many left. McLachlin's report suggested that the early component on the Quillayute System had declined to around 20 percent, and the Commission's own report indicated it was down to 16 percent. The early wild runs on other rivers, especially the smaller ones, have declined even more sharply. On some rivers, they are probably gone.

"Yes, fish are still trickling into the park," Goin said. "And, yes, they are still spawning up there in April. But when my old partner and I were asked to conduct a test fishery up there in 1984, it took us three days to catch a fish. We fished all the old places. They were places that never failed."

All you have to do to gain an understanding of what happened to these fish is read two reports that Jeff Cederholm, a Department of Natural Resources fisheries biologist, submitted to the 1983 Olympic Wild Fish Conference in Port Angeles. In "The Sol Duc River 'Native' Winter-Run Steelhead Project," Cederholm, like Goin, observed that winter steelhead fishing was good on Sol Duc in the 1940s and '50s, with around 1,000 fish taken each year by sport fishermen, mostly by local residents. The fish appeared in late November and ran well into April. They were larger than most steelhead, with fish in the 10- to 12-pound range average and considerable numbers of 20- to 25-pound steelhead. The fish were large, because 35-plus percent of them stayed at sea for three years instead of the more common two years.

According to Cederholm, the Department of Game (DOG) first introduced hatchery steelhead into the Sol Duc in 1953 and began annual plants in 1967. The introduction wasn't because the wild run was in decline; it was simply to provide "more opportunity" for citizens of the state. The stock selected was the state's Chambers Creek stock, which originated in a small south Puget Sound stream and that was first domesticated in the 1920s. "This was a highly cultured strain of relatively small (4-7 pound) steelhead," he wrote. "Due to their early and rather narrow return timing, these hatchery fish were not of high flesh quality for very long after entering freshwater." Nonetheless, these plants had exactly the result that the state desired: Angling pressure increased and the Sol Duc River harvest doubled.

It didn't take long for West End anglers to conclude that the

Chambers Creek fish were a problem. For one thing, the hatchery fish were pretty sorry creatures compared to the 15-, 20- and 25-pound steelhead that the Sol Duc produced naturally. Local anglers also worried that the dramatically increased pressure directed at the hatchery fish would result in an unsustainable incidental harvest of wild Sol Duc steelhead. In the late 1960s, Forks-area sportsmen formed a group, Save Our Native Steelhead, and began to lobby the department and Commission to end the hatchery plants. They eventually succeeded, and the DOG stopped planting Chambers Creek fish in the Sol Duc in 1970.

Then, just when West End anglers assumed that the fishing pressure on the Sol Duc would ease, the 1974 Boldt Decision granted western Washington treaty Indian tribes 50 percent of the harvestable surplus of salmon and steelhead. During its initial years, the Boldt Decision was also interpreted to allow tribal fishermen an unlimited ceremonial harvest on reservations. The Sol Duc and its sister Quillayute System tributaries—the Bogachiel, Calawah and Dickey—don't flow through reservation land. But every fish that eventually returns to these rivers first swims up the Quillayute River, and it does flow past the Quileute Indian Reservation. And since the Bogachiel and Calawah were still heavily planted with early-returning Chambers Creek fish, the tribe logically concentrated its netting during the early season. This subjected the early-timed wild steelhead to an even deadlier gauntlet.

The sport harvest records for the Sol Duc are instructive. From the 1,000 or so wild fish that were annually caught throughout the 1950s, the numbers climbed steeply during the years when both wild and hatchery fish were available. In 1973, the last year there was a full complement of Chambers Creek hatchery fish, anglers harvested 2,500 winter steelhead. The following year, the harvest fell to around 1,200 fish. When you factor in the increased angling pressure and great strides in steelhead tackle that had occurred over the intervening twenty years, it suggests that more anglers were competing for fewer fish. Then, as basically unregulated tribal pressure bore down on the steelhead, the numbers fell even more sharply. In 1976, the number fell to around 600, and by 1977 fewer than 200 fish were recorded by sport fishers. In 1978, the returns were so low the DOG imposed an emergency closure on the Sol Duc in December.

Once again, West End steelheaders responded. This time they formed a Forks chapter of Northwest Steelheaders and developed a plan to restore the dwindling wild run on the Sol Duc. "The program would consist of capturing live adult steelhead," Cederholm wrote. "Progeny of these fish would be reared and returned to the Sol Duc River. After considerable discussion with the Game Department, the native broodstock program was approved." The first returns of these plants returned in 1979. Like the wild Sol Duc fish that they were spawned from, these steelhead contained many 3-salt fish in the 15- to 20-pound class. Meanwhile, the Supreme Court modified the Boldt Decision in 1978 to include fish harvested on reservations in the tribe's share of the fishery. "Since then, there have been credible improvements in catch reporting on both sides, and much better spawning counts," Cederholm wrote.

By the 1980s, the sport harvest on the Sol Duc had climbed back above 2,000, and the escapement was more than 4,000. Since then, wild winter steelhead escapements have been stable, then increased to more than 6,000 fish in the mid-1990s. But the early component of the wild run, the steelhead like those Dick Goin pursued each December, have never recovered. The continuing WDFW policy of intentionally focusing 80 to 90 percent of the winter steelhead harvest on early-returning Chambers Creek fish, ostensibly to protect the late-entry wild fish, ensures that they never will. Even the Washington Fish and Wildlife Commission, which has repeatedly rebuffed attempts to protect these increasingly scarce and threatened fish, grudgingly concedes these policies "may be preventing the rebuilding of the wild early-timed component." The same thing has happened on all major West End rivers.

If you want to know which steelhead life history the WDFW and Commission are turning into ghosts, Jeff Cederholm's second report to the Olympic Wild Fish Conference, "Clearwater River Wild Steelhead Spawn Timing," gives you a good idea. The largest tributary to the Queets River, the Clearwater River drains an area larger than the Bogachiel watershed between the Hoh and Queets basins. Cederholm discovered that the earliest returning Clearwater winter steelhead tended to be tributary spawners. These fish returned to freshwater already "colored up," just like the pink-plated December fish Goin observed on the Sol Duc and

Pysht, and they spawned quickly. This was in striking contrast with later-arriving wild steelhead, which remained bright until late in the season and spawned almost exclusively in the mainstem. It has been suggested that the early spawners utilized the tributaries, because they have more stable flows during the heavy rains of early winter than the mainstems.

In a 1984 presentation to the West End Sportsmen's Club, Cederholm proposed phasing out of the entire Chambers Creek program to protect the beleaguered early wild run. Since then, there has been a swelling chorus of requests for the WDFW and Commission to protect the remnant of wild winter early-return steelhead, either by curtailing the Chambers Creek plants or implementing mandatory wild release during the early season. In 1994, Trout Unlimited called for wild release of all wild steelhead in Boldt Case areas during December and January. Brian McLachlin also submitted his report in support of wild release of early fish in 1994, and Dick Goin make a similar presentation, expanding on McLachlin's report, a few years later.

Olympic National Park has been responsive to concerns about the early run, implementing wild release regulations on the Queets during December and January, as well as year-round wild release on the upper Hoh and Bogachiel. While conceding that previous harvest levels on early-timed steelhead may have altered the historic run timing of West End steelhead, the Commission concluded in 1996 that "recent management plans that focus higher harvest rates on the early-timed portion of the winter steelhead run are not responsible for the shift [in population abundance]. The WDFW still plants virtually all West End rivers that aren't stocked with tribal fish with Chambers Creek steelhead, and it still encourages the harvest of early-timed wild steelhead. During the 1998-99 season, sport fishers killed 184 "unmarked" fish on the Sol Duc, 140 on the Bogachiel, 34 on the Dickey and 34 on the Quillayute between November and the end of January. According to the Commission's logic, this has no affect on the remaining early wild fish.

In addition, the WDFW and Commission are clearly sick of hearing about early-timed steelhead. "They tried to tell me that the fish I was catching on the Sol Duc were summer steelhead," Goin said. "Hell, we don't know why, but the Sol Duc was the worst summer steelhead river on the Olympic Peninsula. If you got a 10-pounder, you talked about it for a week." Despite Cederholm's well-documented research showing early spawning of wild fish on the Clearwater, the WDFW also still characterizes all steelhead that spawn in the State of Washington before March 15 as hatchery fish.

As with all good ghosts, however, the West End rivers' early wild winter steelhead make their presence known just often enough to be inconvenient for the people who would like to forget about them. I took an 18 3/4-pound buck on the Sol Duc a few years ago in mid-January. It was the color of an old brick and was leaking sperm. A couple of years later, I briefly hooked a similarly-sized fish in the same area in December. Its sides were already the color of salmonberry blossoms.

Chapter Six

Bogachiel

Fishing tackle has made dramatic improvements since the first white settlers appeared along West End river valleys in the late 19th Century. This is especially true of fly tackle. But it is hard to imagine a more effective way to fish for steelhead, especially winter steelhead, than the method Chris Morganroth developed on the Bogachiel River in the late 1890s. A German immigrant, Morganroth built the first Bogachiel Valley homestead. Later, he became a Jefferson County constable, the first Forest Service employee on the Olympic Peninsula, and he even traveled to Washington D.C. in the 1930s to lobby for the creation of Olympic National Park. Like most Olympic Peninsula residents then and now, he was also an avid fisherman.

"The Bogachiel, I soon discovered, was a superb fish stream," he wrote in his autobiography, *Footprints in the Olympics*. "Unlike the Hoh and Queets Rivers, which were milky glacier-fed streams, the Bogachiel was clear except for being muddied by a heavy rainfall. No stream in the Olympics can compare with it for fishing, I found the best method for catching the great fighting steelhead was to ride a pony out into the middle of the stream and fish downstream from his back. That way I never had to get wet as the pony was far more sure-footed than I. Fastening the fishline to the saddlehorn was an advantage too."

The Bogachiel River is something of a transitional river, sharing characteristics of both the rainforest rivers to the south and its fellow Quillayute System rivers. In its lower reaches, the Bogachiel features gravel bars and the wide-open feel of a small-scale Hoh or Queets. But it is a snowmelt and rainfall river, without the pulse of glacial run off, and its banks are more stable and it is usually clearer in winter and spring than the rainforest systems. Upstream of the Morganroth Homestead, the forest is huge and primeval, with the streamers of moss and elk-cropped understory that is evocative of the rain forest. But an attentive observer will notice that the Sitka spruce, the dominant tree of the rain forests, is gradually replaced by Douglas fir. Heading up deep in the high country of Olympic National Park, its north and south forks drain a huge area west of Bogachiel Peak and the Bailey Range.

"I was hiking back up into the park and fishing the Bogachiel in 1949 or '50 when no one else did," Dick Goin told me. "Back then, you could drive right to the park boundary at the ranger station." Goin vividly remembers the size of the fish. "One time, my partner and I were idiots and packed four huge fish out," he said, shaking his head at the memory. "It was awful going. It seems like we always got tore out at least once per trip. Some fish we never saw at all. The road fell in a great flood in the 1950s. I hiked up there a few years ago, though, and its still looks pretty wild up there."

Winter steelhead enter the Bogachiel from October into early summer, and they spawn from the lower mainstem up into Olympic National Park. The anadromous fish native to the Bogachiel River are representative of large non-glacial West End systems without large estuaries or lakes. Spring chinook, char and pink and sockeye salmon are basically absent, and chum salmon are present in much smaller numbers than in systems with larger estuaries. Summer chinook are native, however, and its fall chinook were described as one of Washington's healthiest stocks in 1996. Small numbers of summer steelhead reach deep into the Bogachiel backcountry, as do fall coho. But the warm weather fly fishing void left by winter steelhead is filled primarily by sea-run cutthroat trout, which pulse into the river on high tides and rain throughout the summer and fall.

In addition to being a river of transition, the Bogachiel, perhaps more than any other West End river, is a river of contradictions. The lower Bogachiel is one of the easiest and safest rivers to float in a drift or pontoon boat, and it is extremely popular when hatchery fish are returning to the Bogachiel Rearing Pond in December and January. Yet foot access is limited on the lower river and is usually wildly overcrowded when fish are available. Above Highway 101, however, there are miles of hike-in water, and it is relatively lightly fished, even when wild fish return to it in springtime. For fly-fishers, it is also ironic that the drift from the

Bogachiel Rearing Ponds down to the Wilson's Boat Ramp, virtually the domain of bait and hardware steelheaders in the early season, contains some of the best springtime fly water on the Olympic Peninsula.

"I floated the lower Bogey a while ago," said Chris Bellows, skipper of the Neah Bay-based fly-fishing service Topwater Charters and an avid steelhead fly-fisher. "I had forgotten what great fly water it is. There is lots of room, lots of water that is great for swinging a fly. It's big water, perfect for the fly."

The fish that inspect your fly on the Bogachiel are, arguably, the grandest race of winter steelhead in the lower 48 states. Indeed, a 20-plus-pound fish won't even get your name in the paper. That requires a 30-pounder, and several have been landed in recent years. The size of Bogachiel and other Quillayute System winter steelhead is largely the result of their spending more time at sea than any other stock of winter fish. Only slightly more than half of Bogachiel winter steelhead remain at sea for two years. That is the lowest percentage of two-salt fish of any major Northwest river, and the system's 45 percent of three-salts is the highest in Washington, as is its 2 percent of four-salt fish. It also doesn't hurt that, despite the huge infusion of hatchery steelhead into the lower river, the percentage of spawning hatchery fish on the Quillayute System is the lowest in the region.

Chapter Seven

Mr. Glasso's Flies

When you mention the words "steelhead fly" and "Olympic Peninsula" within reasonable proximity to each other, most Northwest fly-fishers automatically think of Syd Glasso. A teacher in the Forks school system for twenty years and a steelhead fly-fisherman with decades of experience on West End rivers, Glasso is best remembered as the creator of the Pacific Northwest's first Spey flies. The elegant, long-hackled patterns of Glasso's Sol Duc and Heron series trace their ancestry to the Atlantic salmon dressings of Scotland's Spey River. While they maintained the basic design of the Scottish flies, he substituted colorful tinsels, fluorescent materials and dyed fur for the somber tones of the originals. Glasso's Spey flies were the first patterns that elevated steelhead fly-tying from the strictly utilitarian to the realm of the aesthetic. Nearly a half-century after developing the Sol Duc Spey and Courtesan and Orange Heron, Glasso's patterns remain the most beautiful winter steelhead flies ever conceived.

They also catch fish. Glasso took first place in the "rainbow" category in the 1958 *Field & Stream* fishing contest with a February 18-pound 12-ounce steelhead that he caught on the Sol Duc with his Sol Duc pattern. That fish was not a fluke, either. "It was nothing for him to fill a punch card," said Dick Wentworth, a friend and fly-fishing and tying protege of Glasso. "And the season only ran to the end of February back then."

Among the fly-fishers who call West End rivers their home waters, Glasso is remembered for much more than just his fly-tying artistry and skill as an angler, though. He is revered as the founder of the region's steelhead fly-fishing heritage. As with his flies, that tradition seems to connect more directly with General Noel Money and Roderick Haig-Brown on Vancouver Island—and through them to Scotland—than with fly-fishing in other areas of the lower 48 states. Indeed, Glasso haunted the Quillayute and rainforest rivers during the years of the Eisenhower presidency with a nine-foot Orvis Battenkill rod, a 3 5/8-ounce Hardy reel and Wheatley fly boxes. He also appears to have been fond of automobiles that were as meticulously crafted as his flies and tackle. "I remember seeing him driving around town in his white Porsche," said well-known fish and wildlife artist Jack Datisman. As befits a teacher, Glasso was a generous angler, fostering the talents of young Forks fly-fishers like Dick Wentworth. His abiding affection for winter steelhead and his early discomfort with killing wild fish have also become the ethical compasses of contemporary Olympic Peninsula fly-fishers.

To get an idea of what an inspired leap Spey flies were, it is necessary to look at the flies that dominated steelhead fly-fishing at the time Glasso designed them. In Joseph D. Bates,' *Streamer Fly Tying and Fishing*, widely-acknowledged as the definitive word on streamer flies when in was first published in 1950 and later updated in 1966, the author discussed steelhead flies at length. The patterns illustrated in its color plates were representative of the era and included the Thor, Bellamy, Black Demon, Royal Coachman, Umpqua Special and Owl Eyed Optic. A. J. McLane's *New Standard Fishing Encyclopedia*, published in 1965 and updated in 1974, added the Skykomish Sunrise, Skunk, Queen Bess, Boss, Burlap and Humboldt Railbird to the canon. With the exception of the Optic and Comets, all of these patterns share the same basic silhouette of the Royal Coachman-inspired patterns that John Benns developed for Eel River steelhead at the turn of the 19th century, and that had evolved into hair wings by the 1930s.

If you hold one of Glasso's patterns, say a Sol Duc Spey, in one hand and a Skykomish Sunrise, probably the most popular winter steelhead fly on Washington rivers between 1940 and 1980, in the other, the differences are striking. The color schemes of the two flies aren't that different; both are dominated by reds, yellows and oranges, the colors at the "bright" winter steelhead end of the spectrum. But the Skykomish Sunrise has distinct boundaries between the different colors, while the Sol Duc Spey colors seem to blend and create a shimmering effect in the water. The lines of the two flies are also markedly different. In keeping with the tradition of the Coachman hair-wings, the Skykomish Sunrise is a compact fly with a cocked wing, and it is tied on a heavy regular hook. Glasso's Sol Duc Spey, on the other hand, reflects the long, low-winged profile of its Scottish inspirations, and Glasso usually tied it on light hooks, rarely larger than size 1.

The behavior of the two flies in the water is as different as their appearance. With its short wing tied in at an acute angle, small body and its heavy hook, the Skykomish Sunrise was designed for large rivers and rough water. In his book on streamers, Bates says that this was in keeping with the basic structural tenets of its era of steelhead flies. " . . . most anglers prefer the high winged bucktail, due to its better action in fast water and because it has less air resistance, allowing it to be cast more easily to the great distances which often are necessary." Bates says that the heavy hook, absorbent materials and compact shape allow the fly to sink quickly in high, fast water. "The fly must sink well down into the water or the fish will not see it," he wrote. "This is particularly true on western steelhead rivers in the winter season . . ." If the Skykomish Sunrise were a horse, it would be a quarter horse—stocky, durable and dependable.

The idea behind the Sol Duc Spey and other Syd Glasso patterns is as different from the Skykomish Sunrise as the original Scottish Spey flies are from classic Atlantic salmon flies. Instead of employing a small, dense design to sink the fly quickly, Glasso created flies that display a proportionally large silhouette but that are actually without much volume. The spare, almost low-water summer steelhead quality of Glasso's winter steelhead flies, combined with the relative lack of buoyancy of the materials he used, are the mechanisms that allowed these flies to sink. They don't sink as quickly as classic steelhead flies like the Skykomish Sunrise, of course, nor do they remain upright in heavy water as well, but they have much more motion, especially in softer water. Glasso Spey flies are leggy, temperamental and gorgeous—they are thoroughbreds.

Although Glasso tied and fished Spey flies with excellent results during the 1950s and '60s, neither was mentioned in Bates' or McClane's books. The first glimpse most steelheaders outside of the West End of the Olympic Peninsula had of the patterns was in the color plates of Trey Combs seminal 1976 volume *Steelhead Fly Fishing and Flies*. Since then, Spey flies have become arguably the most celebrated and most widely imitated steelhead flies throughout the range of *O. mykiss*. Regional and national fly-fishing catalogues now offer dozens of patterns that are clearly inspired by Syd Glasso, and in Combs most recent steelhead book, ***Steelhead Fly Fishing***, dozens of Spey flies are illustrated.

It isn't without some irony, then, that actual Glasso dressings such as the Sol Duc Spey or Orange Heron are almost never available in catalogues or fly shops and few anglers tie them. This is perhaps understandable, because they require uncommon tying skills. They are also time-consuming, and some of the original materials such as heron and seal are now unavailable. Glasso would certainly be surprised if he came back and discovered that most contemporary Spey flies are designed for summer steelhead and the most popular color is purple. Glasso's patterns were designed for winter steelhead, after all. When Trey Combs asked him to suggest flies for summer steelhead on Olympic Peninsula rivers, Glasso didn't even mention one of his flies—he recommended the Royal Coachman! None of Glasso's more celebrated dressings contain purple, either. Its first application in a Spey fly seems to have been in Puget Sound fly-tying master Walter Johnson's, Purple Spey, a fly that he acknowledged was inspired by Glasso.

On the Olympic Peninsula, however, a handful of winter steelhead fly-fishers still pay homage to the Glasso legacy by tying and fishing Spey flies for winter steelhead. Some tie the exact Glasso patterns. They employ substitute materials like schlappen and blue-eared pheasant. Others craft their own dressings in the Glasso tradition. One of the younger generation of West End fly-fishers, John McMillan, ties enormous Spey-influenced flies on 3/0 to 5/0 hooks. His beautiful Claret Caroline and Optimist and Winter's Hope extend Glasso's influence into a second century.

"I'll fish them with clients occasionally," said J.D. Love. "But I mainly fish them personally. I like to fish them in late spring and winter and also quite a bit in the fall. I like them in medium low flows, and in pools and real glassy water. They are not extremely effective in real heavy water."

I have loved Glasso patterns since the first time I saw them, but I had never hooked a winter steelhead with one until a couple of years ago. It was early in the winter, and my wife, Ellie, and I were spending a couple of days at the cabins that the Quileute Tribe rents at La Push. The heavy winter rains that pull hatchery fish upstream and propel boats downstream had yet to materialize. I had gotten up in the dark on our first morning. Stars, which are not a common sight on the beach during winter, flickered overhead, and I had to scrape the truck windshield. I drove over to the confluence of the Bogachiel and Sol Duc at Leyendecker County Park. The ground was frozen when I got out of the truck, and the river was low. It didn't look much different than it had two months earlier, when I had fished it for sea-run cutthroat.

Although Leyendecker is one of the most popular fishing holes on the peninsula, there was no one there that morning—no plunkers, no trailers, not even any evidence of tribal nets. The lower Sol Duc is easier to fly-fish than the Bogey, so I angled off under the new bridge and followed the trail by the cow pasture. The stars had faded by now, and it was light enough to see the path. I was very careful about keeping myself and my graphite rod, which I have been told is a good conductor of electricity, away from the cattle fence. I haven't been knocked to the ground by an electric fence since I was a kid, but I remember the sensation clearly. I passed the first couple of places where you can scoot down to the river and fish from the rip rap.

I have heard many times over the years that the riffle above the mouth of the Sol Duc was one of Syd Glasso's favorite places to fish. Recently, a friend of mine told me that Glasso actually preferred a drift farther upstream, near the first bend in the river. But I know the layout of the rocks and snags in the area above the mouth better, and I clambered down to the water and took up position on a large flat boulder. It was noticeably colder next to the river, like opening the door of a refrigerator's freezer compartment. I zipped up the front of my fleece jacket, and opened my winter steelhead fly box.

Maybe it was the combination of seeing a low and moderately flowing river and knowing that Syd Glasso had fished this stretch of the Sol Duc regularly, but my eyes were immediately drawn to a Spey fly. It was an Orange Heron, tied on a size-1 hook. It had been a present from a friend. As its name suggests, heron was featured prominently in the original pattern, in this case as a wing. My friend substituted stripped marabou for the palmered hackle along the body. He also used goat in place of the seal. Despite the improvised nature of the materials, it looked to my eyes very much like the Orange Heron that Glasso tied for the color plate in Combs' early book.

I decided to work the pocket water below my rock perch first. I began with a few roll casts. I let the fly sink, then tried to draw it slowly, enticingly through the broken water. It was just beginning to be light enough to see the hint of green in the river when I approached the limit of my roll-casting ability. I stripped a couple more feet of line and cast conventionally, across and downstream. The fly landed a few feet inside the seam between the main channel and the pocket water. I tossed an upstream loop, then reached out with my rod, trying to extend the swing as long as I could. I felt the hit just as the fly began to hang downstream. It felt like a heavy fish.

I didn't land that steelhead, didn't even get a chance to play it. It came out of the water, heavy and ponderous, revealing the thick swimmer's shoulders of Sol Duc natives. It was a big fish, probably at least 15 pounds. In the early half-light, it looked perfectly black and white, like an old photograph taken in the days before color. It jumped again, a slow motion half turn and writhed powerfully. The leader snapped audibly.

Suddenly, a horn honked. Looking downstream, I saw a large pickup on the bridge. Its lights were on and I could see the exhaust trailing behind. It flashed its lights. The driver must have stopped to look at the river and happened to see the fish jump. I waved my rod. The driver honked again, then drove west, towards the beach.

I stripped the line in slowly, my mind utterly blank. Although I had lost the fish, I was happy, flush with the glow of having accomplished something, something that feels important. I stood on the rock for several minutes, without any words entering my mind. The first intelligible thought that flickered across my consciousness was that Syd Glasso may have stood on this same spot more than half a century ago.

It's hard not to think of Syd Glasso when you cast flies for winter steelhead on Olympic Peninsula rivers.

Chapter Eight

Deus Ex Machina

Two thousand yeas ago, the ancient Greek dramatists—Aeshylus, Sophocles and Euripides—occasionally wrote themselves into a bind. The plots of their plays were dictated by tradition and myth, and the audiences knew the stories of Oedipus and Agamemnon and Midea intimately. So the authors expressed their creativity by tinkering with the edges of the narrative, by character development and by exploring complex social issues. But even these great tragedians wrote themselves into a corner from time to time. When that happened, the playwrights simply had an actor representing one of the Greek gods appear on stage atop a mechanical device and tidy up the story. This intervention came to be known as the ***Deus Ex Machina***. It translates as "The God from the Machine."

At the beginning of the 20th century, West Coast fish managers and the politicians who funded them found themselves in a similarly impossible quandary. From the massive Columbia River to small creeks, the Pacific Northwest's once seemingly inexhaustible salmon and trout runs were in obvious and alarming decline. The reasons for the decline, although not widely appreciated by the public at the time, were understood by biologists. The collapse of Atlantic salmon on the East Coast was a recent and compelling cautionary tale. "It was the mills, the dams, the steamboats, the manufacturers injurious to the water, and similar causes, which, first making the stream more and more uninhabitable for the salmon, finally exterminated them altogether," Livingstone Stone wrote in the ***Transactions of the American Fisheries Society*** in 1892. But the prevailing social and economic ethos at the time was still based upon a relentless exploitation of natural resources and the conversion of fish and wildlife habitat to private property.

The God From the Machine the late 19th century fish managers came up with, of course, was the fish hatchery.

"Hatcheries didn't derive from any scientific basis," Jim Lichatowich told me. "They didn't know enough then. But hatcheries were consistent with the development ideology of the time. There is a role for hatcheries, but, boy, they need a major overhaul. They have failed."

On the Olympic Peninsula, hatcheries arrived later than in most areas of the Pacific Northwest. The first was a federal facility on Lake Quinault in 1916, built over the objections of the Quinault Tribe. Compared to Puget Sound, the Willamette Valley and lower Columbia, and the Columbia and Snake rivers, the impact of hatcheries on West End rivers, has been far less profound. But you don't have to wander far on these rivers before you encounter a hatchery or rearing facility, and there are currently no major rivers that don't receive some sort of hatchery plant. Pacific salmon account for much of this production, but steelhead are released by the WDFW; by the Makah, Quiluete, Hoh and Quinault tribes; and by private organizations and the federal government. According to the most recent WDFW Steelhead Harvest Reports, more than one million winter steelhead are released annually in rivers between the Lyre and Quinault.

In his celebrated analysis of the salmon crisis, *Salmon Without Rivers*, Jim Lichatowich argues that the fundamental problem plaguing Northwest salmon and steelhead today is the conflict between the "natural economy" and the "industrial economy." Wild salmonids, he maintains, evolved under a natural economy in which a diversity of life histories within individual populations served as insurance against floods and droughts, earthquakes and volcanoes, and fluctuating ocean conditions. The natural economy was a complex, inter-related mosaic, characterized by interspecies dependencies, abundance and nutrient recycling. The industrial economy that Euro-American conquerors imposed on top of the natural economy, on the other hand, demanded simplicity, technology and constant attention from human beings. The title of Jim's book is an ironic reference to the assumption that hatcheries would allow intensive fisheries to continue in the face of widespread habitat degradation.

"We assumed we could make salmon so abundant we wouldn't have to worry about harvest or habitat," he told me. "We bet the farm on that assumption and the huge number of species on the

Endangered Species list is a clear indication that we lost that bet."

Obviously, distributing a handful of steelhead broodstocks throughout the region is as clear an example of the industrial economy at work as you are going to find. Like the Douglas fir tree farms that have replaced actual forests and the dredged, filled and bulkheaded waterfronts that replace salt marshes and estuaries, Chambers Creek winter steelhead are a perfect expression of the values of the industrial economy. Because they returned early and over a narrow period of time, they were easy for hatchery managers, who prefer to attain their allotted spawner numbers as early as possible. They were convenient for biologists, too, because their early timing allowed managers to, theoretically, manage them as an entirely different species than wild fish. Chambers Creek fish also fulfilled the primary function in the industrial economy—they were cheap. Instead of investing money and time in creating river-specific winter steelhead runs, they let managers, literally, produce virtually uniform, assembly-line steelhead.

The Olympic Peninsula, as was noted in an earlier chapter, was one of the first places where anglers rebelled against hatchery steelhead. Initially, concerns centered around the intense pressure directed at early-returning Chambers Creek fish and fears that it would result in an unsustainable harvest of wild steelhead on the Quillayute System and other rivers. But in time, anglers began to raise other questions. Like their counterparts throughout the Northwest, many Olympic Peninsula anglers claimed that hatchery fish didn't fight either as hard or as long as wild steelhead. The strangely cyclical, boom-and-bust nature of the returns, which contrasted dramatically with the stable or increasing wild run on West End rivers in the 1990s, also suggested rather starkly that hatchery steelhead were less hardy than wild fish. During the 1997-98 winter steelhead season, hatchery returns to the Bogachiel Rearing Pond collapsed to the point that the WDFW imposed an emergency closure on recreational harvest.

"During the same year, the wild winter steelhead return was strong," Peter Bahls wrote in "How Healthy are Healthy Stocks?" "with over 12,352 wild fish, suggesting that the resilience of hatchery fish under fluctuating ocean conditions may be substantially lower than that of wild fish."

If hatchery fish aren't as fit at surviving in the wild as native stocks, that raised an obvious question: What happens when hatchery fish spawn with wild fish? The WDFW's predecessor agencies had always claimed that this was rare, that there was little contact between wild and Chambers Creek fish on the spawning grounds. Indeed, even today the agency maintains that hatchery steelhead spawn before March 15, and wild fish spawn after that date. But those assurances began to ring hollowly in the 1970s after technology that allowed biologists to genetically investigate different stocks of steelhead became available. These early analyses indicated that wild steelhead from West End rivers were, indeed, still more closely related to one another than to steelhead from Puget Sound or neighboring regions. But the stocks demonstrated considerably less genetic variability than steelhead populations on Vancouver Island. Since Vancouver Island streams had received few hatchery steelhead at that time, it suggested that hatchery fish had spawned with wild Olympic Peninsula stocks.

Then in 1994, the late Steve Phelps and four other WDFW biologists released "Genetic Analyses of Washington Steelhead." Among other things, it compared the genetic distance between Chambers Creek hatchery steelhead and wild Olympic Peninsula steelhead taken in the 1970s with new collections of wild fish that were obtained in the early 1990s. The samples from the rivers that drain into the western Strait of Juan de Fuca, collections from the Pysht, Lyre, and East Twin, had become markedly more similar to Chambers Creek steelhead over the subsequent 20 years. Only the Hoko and Deep Creek collections had become less similar to Chamber Creek fish, and this was almost certainly attributable to the fact that their hatchery stock was from the Quinault Indian Fish Hatchery. Of the streams that flow into the Pacific Ocean, the steelhead from the Bogachiel Rearing Pond ranked just below Tokul Creek Hatchery (a tributary to the Snoqualmie River) and just above the mainstem Skykomish River stock as the closest genetically to Chambers Creek hatchery fish. In other words, the steelhead that annually draw hundreds of anglers to remote West End rivers each December are a lot closer genetically to the fish that swim beneath the Tacoma Narrows Bridge than the steelhead that evolved in Olympic Peninsula rivers.

There were also encouraging glimpses of wild steelhead populations that seemed to be holding their own. Earlier collections from the Dickey River had revealed a unique genetic marker found in none of the other samples, as had samples from the Ozette River. Steelhead from Sitkum River, a tributary to the South Fork of the Calawah River, deviated the most widely from Chambers Creek hatchery steelhead of any Quillayute System fish sampled. That suggested that at least some wild tributary spawners were still not only managing to avoid tribal nets on the Quillayute and the increasingly intense sport fishery on the Bogachiel and Calawah, but also finding one another on the spawning grounds. To the south, the Hoh, Queets and Quinault rivers have been heavily planted in recent years, but the broodstocks employed are for the most part native to these rivers.

Of course, not a few people consider concerns over the genetics of steelhead and other salmonids as pointless exercises in self indulgence. "There are no wild fish anymore," they never tire of repeating. It is an article of faith among these folks that decades of hatchery plants have obliterated any semblance of native stocks, and they insist wild and hatchery fish should be managed identically. In 1999, a coalition of homebuilders, realtors, and the agriculture lobby sued the National Marine Fisheries Service (NMFS) for not counting hatchery fish in its deliberations over whether to list Puget Sound chinook salmon as "threatened" under the Endangered Species Act. Two years later, John Hogan, a conservative federal judge with a record of sympathy toward property rights activists ruled that it had been illegal for NMFS to exclude hatchery coho from protections applied to wild Oregon Coast coho because the agency had included them in the same Evolutionarily Significant Unit. Within weeks of the Hogan Decision, NMFS received petitions to "delist" seven stocks of Columbia/Snake river salmon and steelhead.

However, the people who had studied Pacific salmon the longest weren't buying the farmers' and developers' and dam operators' version of fisheries biology. "Each river and tributary has a discrete strain of fish, adapted through generations of natural selection to the local habitat and environment," Jim Lichatowich wrote in support of a stay of the Hogan Decision while it was under appeal "... a growing body of scientific evidence has documented the threats that hatchery fish pose to wild salmon populations. These threats fall broadly into three categories: 1) threats to genetic diversity and population fitness; 2) ecological threats; and 3) threats from fisheries that target mixed hatchery and wild stocks."

Jeff Cederholm, the DNR biologist who researched wild steelhead on the Sol Duc and Clearwater rivers in the 1980s and who was recently the lead author of "Pacific Salmon and Wildlife," an exhaustive study on the role of nutrients in salmon productivity, dismissed the arguments of hatchery advocates out of hand. "I think we should unilaterally get rid of any semblance of artificial production and put the money we're spending on hatcheries into restoring natural production," he said. "The money invested in hatcheries has been a waste of money. It gives a false perception of abundance and takes money away from habitat protection. I can't believe with the level of science we have now, we continue to perpetuate artificial production."

Not all anglers, not even all fly-fishers, are ready to go that far. On the Olympic Peninsula, the guides' association and volunteers have devoted thousands of hours to the Snyder Creek Hatchery operation. It is a revived version of the original Sol Duc brood program in the 1980s, and it spawns only wild Sol Duc steelhead that return early in the season. It currently releases around 100,000 smolt annually. After extremely poor returns during the 1990s, it has begun to contribute to the sport catch. "My clients caught about 25 last year," J.D. Love told me in the autumn of 2001. "They came between mid-December and mid-January. That's what they are designed to do." Hatcheries founded on local broodstocks have been developed in other areas, as well, and such operations can have river-specific goals and schedules, even decommissioning dates. Although the record has been mixed, hatcheries can protect the genetic legacies of seriously endangered populations by breeding the surviving fish in captivity.

There is something truly squalid and pathetic about the very enterprises that brought about the perceived need for hatcheries in the first place now insisting on their right to continue their second century of assault on salmonid habitat because, in their view, there are now no longer any wild fish. Certainly, some populations have been genetically compromised, even overwhelmed—Puget sound coho and upper Columbia River steelhead come to mind. A report commissioned by the Lower Elwha S'Klallam Tribe in 1996 indicated that hatchery practices had contributed to the decline of wild coho in the Sooes, Waatch, Sail, Pysht, Deep and East and West Twin rivers. Anyone who claims that there are no wild winter steelhead left on the Olympic Peninsula has spent a lot more time rooting around in the Industrial Economy than they have on the water.

I will never forget the last time I fished the lower Bogachiel during the hatchery run. It was December, a week or so before Christmas, and Jay Brevik, Marshall Ross and I wanted a few steelhead for the holidays. We hooked the first fish of the day only a couple hundred yards below the hatchery ramp. Marshall beached the boat on a gravel bar, and for the next hour he gave a clinic in bait fishing. All of the steelhead were under eight pounds or so, and they were all as bright as new nails.

Then Marshall hollered that he had a heavier fish. I laid my rod on the rocks and ran over to watch. The steelhead didn't jump, but instead peeled line quickly from the reel. It ran far downstream, finally stopping in the soft water along the bank, outside the main current. In order to bring it to hand, Marshall had to work it back across the heavier water below the bar. It was a strong fish, much stronger than the steelhead we had been catching, and used the current seam to its advantage. It took quite a while to work it back upstream.

I got my first good look at the steelhead when Marshall held it in his palm as he removed the hook. It was about 12 pounds and was a thick-shouldered fish, almost like a coho. Its back was a vivid green, peppered with black spots, and its gill plates and sides were splashed with red. Only about 10 miles from the ocean, it already looked like a summer steelhead in the headwaters in October.

The God From the Machine had nothing to do with that fish.

Chapter Nine

Winter Solstice

When you are fly-fishing for winter steelhead and things aren't working out the way you planned, sometimes the most sensible thing to do is throw in the towel. Any number of things can doom a steelhead trip on the Olympic Peninsula. Rivers that were dropping and clearing at twilight can flow up in the alders after a night of rain. An upstream mudslide can turn a clear river into a muddy torrent. Sometimes the fish won't bite. Other times there doesn't seem to be any in the river. If you are touchy and territorial like me, you can also become disgusted if the river is too crowded. You might move to two or three other spots, but eventually you just shrug and mutter, "The hell with it."

Pulling the plug on an outing is simple when you are wade fishing a short distance from your car: You break your rod down, hike back through the woods to the road, and head for the Sappho Cafe or Westward Hoh for a cup of coffee. It is more complicated in a drift boat or raft, because once you float out of sight of the ramp you are locked into the entire drift. It is also more difficult to quickly abandon a fishing trip when you have hiked a considerable distance from the road, my preferred way of fishing. But the absolute worst situation to find yourself in when the fishing goes south is on a backpacking trip into a remote area. On a short winter day, there usually isn't enough daylight left to make it back to your car by the time you figure out that you aren't going to catch any fish.

I don't remember exactly when the idea to fish the mouth of the Ozette River on the Winter Solstice occurred to me. The three-mile hike from the Lake Ozette Ranger Station to Cape Alava, the westernmost point in the contiguous United States, has always been one of my favorite hikes. The sea stacks and islets, the Indian petroglyphs and sea birds, the windrows of drift logs and rafts of kelp all combine to make Cape Alava one of the most stunning places on the Pacific coast. I had hiked from the cape up to the mouth of Ozette River many times over the years, and had even tried fishing it once for cutthroat. At some point, I decided I wanted to try to catch an Ozette River winter steelhead from its estuary.

The allure of the trip was clear—steelhead with the raw energy and color of a breaking wave, in a gorgeous setting, and without even the prospect of another angler or tribal net. But I must admit that the idea of fishing the river on December 21, the Winter Solstice, was more fanciful. There was something irresistible about the notion of carrying my old Kelty pack out to the western crust of the continent and contemplating the darkest day of the year from that rocky promontory. I don't think I expected that such a gesture would produce a life-altering insight, but I figured that at the very least it would be interesting and something to tell people about later.

Two or three Winter Solstices came and went before I actually drove out to the coast. I planned to hike the three miles to the cape in the late morning, set up camp, then walk up the two miles of beach to the river during the middle of the day. The highest tide of the day always occurs during the daytime in winter, and that day it was at 12:30 in the afternoon. I had no clear idea what phase of the tide would be the best to fish the river mouth, but I reasoned that fish that swam into the lower tidal pools on the head of the tide might tend to remain as it ebbed. Because solstice tides are the highest of the year, I figured that the surf would prevent me from even reaching the river until at least a couple of hours after the tide turned. At best, I would have about an hour to fish, then would have to hurry back to my tent before it got dark at around 4:30.

The forecast called for rain, but it was a typically damp overcast day in the low 50s when I turned off Highway 112 onto the Hoko-Ozette Road. By the time I pulled into the parking lot at the ranger station, however, the western horizon had taken on a grayish-purple bruised look. The tops of the conifers were swaying and crows wheeled on a freshening breeze. It looked as though something big was blowing in. For a moment, I thought about changing my plans. I could have easily gotten into the truck, driven back to the Hoko. I could have fished its fly-only water for a few hours, then driven home and slept in my bed. But I felt committed. I wriggled into my pack, signed in at the ranger station kiosk and stepped onto the Ozette River bridge.

Located just downstream of the river's outlet on Lake Ozette, the bridge is the only place where you can see the river from a trail. After the bridge, the river winds to the northwest through virtually impenetrable coastal forest, while the Sand Point and Cape Alava trails, the two trails that lead to the beach, trend vaguely to the south and west. During the summer and autumn, the time of year most hikers see the river, it is low and the color of weak iced-tea. Even now, more than a month into the rainy season, the river was higher but still carried the cedar-stain. Although the entire reach of the Ozette River and Lake Ozette's shoreline are protected within Olympic National Park, all of the rivers that feed the lake flow through private industrial timberlands, and they are some of the most degraded land on the peninsula. Lake Ozette sockeye salmon are currently on the federal list of endangered species, and its chinook, coho and steelhead populations have all been affected by the poor habitat.

It wasn't only logging that damaged the Ozette basin's steelhead and salmon. "In 1952, 26 large log jams were removed from the river," Olympic National Park fisheries biologist, John Meyer, told me. "It had an effect on the lake level (it lowered it) and probably had a real effect on steelhead, cutthroat and sockeye. Then they moved up to Big River. We know now that's about the worst thing that can be done to a river."

I stared at the river for a few minutes, then proceeded to the fork in the trail. I headed right, on the Cape Alava Trail. Unlike most trails in the Olympics, the two trails to the beach are boardwalks, built from cedar puncheons. This allows you to walk above the great morass of mud and puddles and muck that cover the ground here most of the year. The boardwalk can be slippery, especially in winter, and I was wearing soft-soled running shoes rather than my hiking boots, as the park recommends. It took me a while to adjust to the weight of the pack and the unyielding nature of the cedar planks, but I soon succumbed to that rhythmic, hypnotic hiking stride that I have loved since I was a kid.

As always, I was struck by how different the coastal forest looked from either the rainforest valleys or the Douglas fir woods of the upper Sol Duc and Bogachiel. For one, there is an immense amount of blowdown and sheared off tree-tops. That is the result of the hurricane-force winds that shriek through these woods about every 20 years. The understory is also much more densely vegetated, with incredible tangles of salal, berries and brush, much of it towering over the head of a man. In *Olympic Battleground*, Carsten Lien's excellent history of the struggle to preserve portions of Olympic Peninsula forests from the timber industry, he attributes this to the slaughter of Ozette area elk in the 1890s.

"At that time, the Ozette forest had the open understory characteristic of the Hoh valley today," he wrote. "In an operation as ruthless as the slaughtering of the buffalo of the Great Plains, hide and teeth hunters moved into the area and killed most of the herd. Hides to be tanned for leather were shipped out by sailing schooner from a trading post at the mouth of the Ozette River. Walter Ferguson, who operated the trading post, reported with pride that he was able to kill seventy elk in a single day out of a band of 250 sighted at Swan Bay. The few surviving elk that were not killed later by Ozette homesteaders were doomed by the blowdown of 1921, which marooned them and blocked their accustomed trail. With the elk gone, the Ozette forest reverted to the impassable tangle of understory which remains today."

The first spatters of rain snapped me out of my reverie on the elk. The sky had become a solid bank of gray now, and clouds were moving inland quickly, not much above the treetops. The wind was stiffer too, with gusts that bent the treetops as though they were no more resistant than a field of hay. I thought again about turning back, but at this point I had a certain momentum going. I stopped briefly and put on my light rain anorak when the rain began to come down harder. I took a break at Ahlstrom's Prairie, the homestead of an early pioneer who lived alone on the coast for more than 50 years. For the first time, it occurred to me that a heavy, storm-driven surf might prevent me from even reaching the mouth of the river.

I could hear the pounding of the surf farther inland than usual, even over the wind. Despite that rather alarming portent, I was totally unprepared for the sight that I beheld when I topped the final rise above the beach. Stretching as far as I could see into the rain-obscured murk, the ocean was a white-crested maelstrom. Large waves smashed against Ozette Island directly offshore.

Spray climbed up its sides, then collapsed back in sheets of foam. The surf near the shore was a soup of whitewater, drift logs and kelp. Water covered the campsites closest to the beach, and trees creaked wildly in the woods. It was 12:20, a few minutes before high tide.

The smart thing, obviously, would have been to turn around. It was clear that the storm was not just a squall line but extended many miles out to sea. I realized that the waves were going to take a long time to play themselves out, and that I wouldn't have a chance to see the Ozette River on this trip. It occurred to me that I could make it back to the ranger station by 2:00, to Sekiu by 3:00, and back home in Port Townsend in time for a late supper. But, as I said, the fishing trip had only been part of the appeal of this trip. I was still intrigued by the idea of spending the longest night of the year on this remote outpost. I also knew that, just as the highest tides of the year occur during the daytime at the solstice, the lowest, conversely, happen at night. I figured I would be safe once the tide began to peel back.

So I stayed put. I sat on the wooden steps that lead to the beach for several hours. For many people, that might seem incredible, to simply sit and watch the rain and waves, but I am a duck hunter and bow hunter as well as a steelhead fisherman, and that is pretty much a job description for those activities. Besides, I like storms. I love the fact that they rend the fabric of the day and liberate you from normal concerns. I heard a few trees splinter, then crash in the distance, but it eventually quit raining and the wind began to die down. A short time before dusk, which was even earlier than usual because of the cloud cover, I noticed that more of the beach was above water. The tide had begun to turn, despite the surging waves. I climbed down the steps to the beach.

The intertidal zone was a chaotic jumble of wood chips, probably spilled from an offshore barge, tree limbs and beach logs. There was also all of the human detritus that perennially decorates Northwest beaches—pieces of net, ropes from ships, different colored Styrofoam blocks, crab floats and the, always inexplicable, sodden articles of clothing, especially tennis shoes. But the forest above the beach looked as though it had been above water all afternoon. It wasn't exactly dry, but there wasn't any standing water. I set up camp quickly next to an old fire ring. I knew there would be another high tide around midnight, but it was a couple of feet less than the daytime high. Unless the weather actually got worse, I figured I would be fine.

Now, I may very well be a moron for having pushed on toward the coast on that stormy December day, but I have camped out for a lot of years, and I at least know the things that make life bearable on a long night in the woods. So after I scraped out the fire ring, I crawled into the tent and removed them from my backpack. First and probably foremost, was my down vest. I shucked my anorak and snapped up the vest. I felt cozier already. Then I retrieved the candle lantern. I slipped its hook through the loop at the top of the tent's interior. Knowing that I would be able to read my way through the long evening lifted my spirits even farther. Below that, were three pieces of cedar kindling and two pieces of firewood. I had seen the forecast for rain, and since a short overnight didn't require a lot of food or clothes, I had packed the wood. There was also a Ross MacDonald mystery, Lew Archer's *The Way Some People Die*, and a half-full pint bottle of Christian Brothers brandy.

It was a little early for a snort, so I grabbed my flashlight. I knew my firewood wasn't going to last very long, and I thought I might be able to find some dry heartwood in a snag. Basically, it was something to do. The beam of my light wasn't very wide, though, and walking was tricky on the wet branches. Realizing that this would be an extremely inopportune time to break a bone, I headed back toward camp. Then my light reflected something shiny, something that looked man-made, leaning up against a tree near another old campsite. Moving closer, I saw that it was a plastic garbage bag. I had an idea of what was under the bag, and when I lifted it up it was, indeed, wood. It wasn't completely dry—who knows how long it had been there?—but when I hefted a piece it was light, not waterlogged. Even better, it was cedar.

My dry wood from home caught quickly, and soon orange flames cast shadows beneath the trees. I laid a couple of pieces of my found wood up against the flame to dry, and began messing around with my dinner. It consisted of a Styrofoam container of noodle soup, the kind you add boiling water to, along with a hunk of cheese and a tin of Vienna sausages. I filled my sauce pan with water from my Nalgene bottle, and balanced it over two parallel logs. I splashed an inch or two of brandy into my enameled blue cup.

The only way to reach Cape Alava and most of Olympic National Park's 57-mile coastal strip is by foot. The longest stretch of wilderness sea coast in the lower 48 states, its rocky points, cobble beaches, and creek mouths support seabird colonies, teeming tide pools and the largest concentration of sea otters in Washington. Its offshore waters, where gray whales appear seasonally and where coastal upwelling creates one of the richest marine habitats in the world, are now protected by the 2,500-square-mile Olympic Coast National Marine Sanctuary. Its inshore kelp beds are the thickest on the planet, and they support myriad species of bottomfish, as well as provide cover for juvenile salmonids. Within more protected coves, eel grass beds nourish shellfish and fin fish. The sandy beaches where the eel grass thrives are, in turn, maintained by the plume of sand from the Columbia River, which drifts all the way up to the coastal strip in winter. In yet another example of their seemingly endless tentacles of destruction, however, recruitment of sand on coastal beaches has declined by between 24 and 50 percent since the construction of the Columbia and Snake river dams.

Today, hikers and backpackers are the only human beings along the coastal wilderness. But, as my cedar logs sparked and crackled in the darkness, I remembered that many of these beaches had once been the sites of tribal villages. Indeed, the Ozette Indians lived in permanent cedar longhouses at Cape Alava for thousands of years before European explorers arrived in the 18th century. Closely related to the Makah by ancestry and language, they hunted whales, fished for salmon and halibut, and hunted bear and elk. They carved the drawings of sailing ships and fish and birds at Wedding Rock, a mile to the south. They also traded the prized sockeye that swam up the Ozette River with other tribes, and they maintained camas prairies above the beach with controlled burning. Some anthropologists believe that the Ozette and other coastal native societies had a more prosperous standard of living than their 16th- and 17th-century European counterparts.

Perhaps it was the darkness or the booze, but I couldn't keep my thoughts from the ultimate fate of the Ozette. They were one of the first Olympic Peninsula tribes to have contact with European sailing ships, and in 1799 they became one of the first to contract and die from smallpox. Even more devastating smallpox outbreaks followed, as well as equally deadly influenza, measles, tuberculosis and other epidemics. In *The Land of the Quinault*, the Quinault Tribe's superb history of its people, it was suggested that the tribal societies the first overland settlers encountered in the 1850s were but fragmented remnants, faint echoes of pre-contact cultures. I wondered if the impenetrable brush on the Ozette uplands today reflects not only the loss of elk but also the contagion that left the tribe too weak to tend to its camas prairies. At any rate, the last Ozette abandoned Cape Alava in the 1920s, after the federal government insisted that its children attend school in Neah Bay. In a particularly ghastly way, Cape Alava's original human culture collapsed even before the river's sockeye or Ozette's elk and forests.

Those weren't exactly the sort of insights I had in mind when I decided to make my solstice pilgrimage to Cape Alava. Shaking myself to exorcise the ghosts, I stood up and walked toward the black water. I hadn't noticed it while I was beside the fire, but there were patches of clear sky now. Low white clouds scudded before a higher denser blanket of gray, but every once in a while an opening would appear in the clouds. I would briefly see stars, pulsing against an inky background, then they would vanish. The tide was well off the beach now, and I savored the rich iodine smell of the intertidal zone.

Eventually, I walked back to camp. I held my hands over the coals for a couple of minutes, then crawled into the tent. I lit the candle lantern and pulled the sleeping bag up around my shoulders like a shawl. I opened the paperback and quickly immersed myself in 1960s Los Angeles, into the world of troubled teenagers and women with secrets and rich men who only loved themselves. It was hard to believe that Lou Archer's and my worlds existed on the same ocean—as it was even harder to believe that this remote beach once rang with voices that are now silent.

I looked at the bottle. It had about two fingers left in it, "What the hell," I thought, as I tipped it up.

It was the longest night of the year, after all.

Black and Blue Spey Grub
Tied by John Alevras

Black Gordon
Tied by John McMillan

Blue Fox Tail Tube
Tied by John Alevras

Bobbie Jean
Tied by Chuck Cameron

Brown Heron
Tied by Chuck Cameron

Kate
Tied by Chuck Cameron

Lady Claret Caroline
Tied by John McMillan

Orange Black Olympic Stone
Tied by Chuck Cameron

Orange Heron
Tied by Chuck Cameron

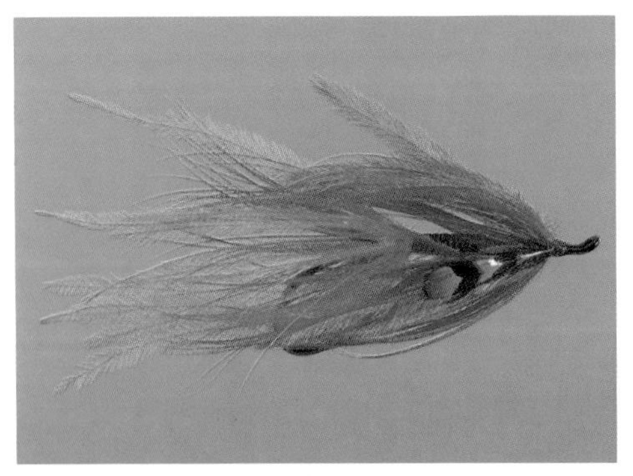

Orange Spey Grub
Tied by John Alevras

Orange Trinity
Tied by Chuck Cameron

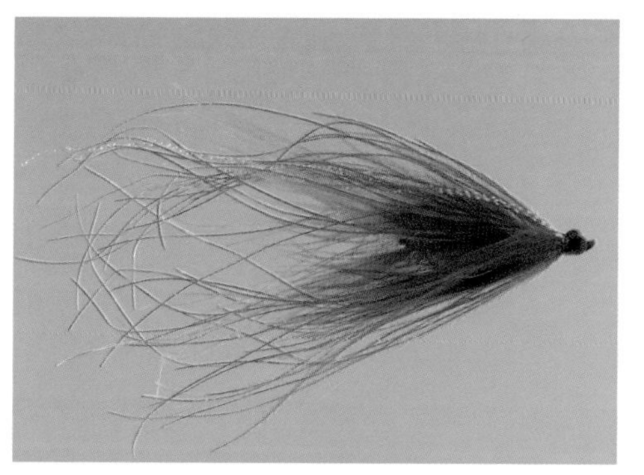

Peninsula Squid
Tied by John McMillan

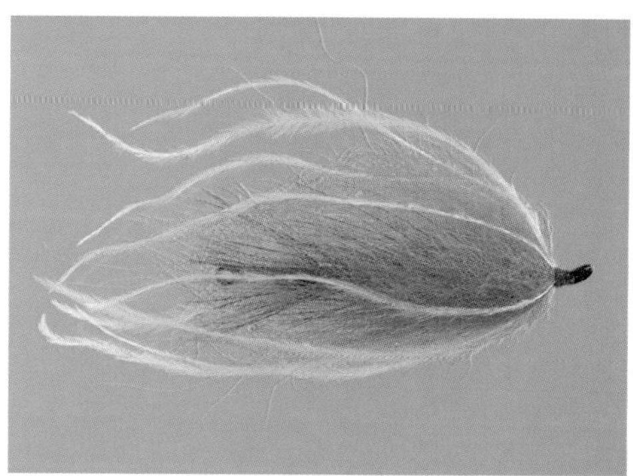

PO Shank Fly
Tied by Dave Steinbaugh

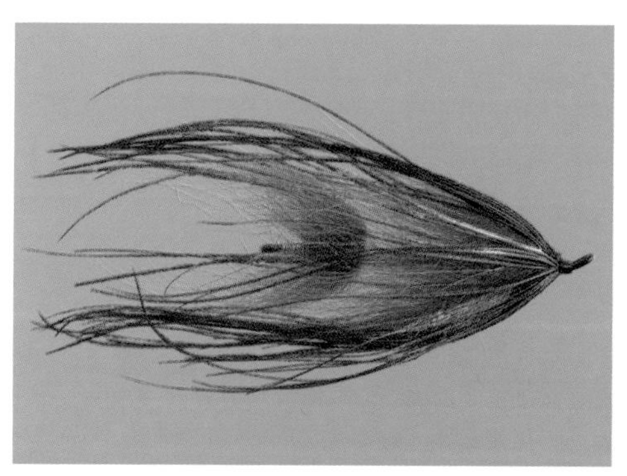

Purple Shank Fly
Tied by Dave Steinbaugh

Sol Duc
Tied by Chuck Cameron

Sol Duc Spey
Tied by John McMillan

Winter's Hope
Tied by John McMillan

Calawah River

Hoh River

Resident rainbows are genetic-diversity insurance for wild steelhead.

Twenty-eight-inch wild Bogachiel hen taken in April.

Fly-only water on the upper Hoh River in Olympic National Park.

Wild January 36x21-inch Sol Duc buck.

Jim Kerr with a bright Hoh River steelhead. Photo by Jim Kerr

Ten miles from the road in Olympic National Park. Photo by Doug Rose

Pteronarcys californica water in spring on the upper Sol Duc.

Wild Salmon Center refugia in Hoh basin.

Fly Fisher's Fantasy, painting by Jack Datisman.

Twenty-nine-inch wild Sol Duc hen ready to spawn in mid-December.

Spey-rod water on the Bogachiel.

Alder bottom on the Queets
Photo by Doug Rose

Chapter Ten

Hoh

The Hoh has always been a river of boats. For centuries, the Hoh Indians traveled between their upriver hunting camps and downstream fishing villages in shovel-nosed canoes made from cedar or Sitka spruce. When the first settlers, the Andersons on the lower Hoh and the Heulsdonks on the upper river, arrived in the late 1890s, they adopted their neighbors' method of travel. Paddling when they were traveling downstream and standing up and using poles when they needed to buck the current, the settlers became excellent boatmen and were often employed to ferry school teachers and haul supplies. Boats became less critical after the Highway 101 bridge spanned the river in the 1930s, and roads now penetrate the north and south banks above and below the bridge. But boats are still the best way to get around on the Hoh, and today just about every boat on the river during winter contains anglers pursuing steelhead.

Actually, Hoh valley pioneers didn't bother with steelhead much. Lena Fletcher, the daughter of the legendary Iron Man of the Hoh, John Heulsdonk, wrote about her life on the upper Hoh for years in the Forks newspaper. She recalled that she and her three sisters were all pressed into fishing to enhance the family's basic larder of elk and venison, grouse and berries and garden vegetables. Her mother had the girls concentrate on cutthroat trout, "Dolly Varden" and whitefish. According to Fletcher, the steelhead were too much for their tackle, and fall salmon were not considered in good eating shape once they had reached that high in the river.

"We began going out there off and on by the early 1950s," Dick Goin told me. "I think we saw the first drift boats in 1956. Before that, we were going downstream in inflatables, war surplus rafts. My partner and I did between half and two-thirds of our fishing in rafts. Occasionally someone would have a homemade wood boat. But it was usually a one-trip-and-swim-to-shore kind of deal. The lower river was open in spring, and there were lots of bright fish. They were grand sport. One time three of us took a limit of three each and it took four gunny sacks for the nine fish. Only one sack would hold three fish."

Today, most people think of the Hoh as consisting of three sections—the upper and lower Hoh, separated by the Highway 101 bridge, and the park water upstream. Painted with bold brush strokes on a massive canvas, the lower and upper Hoh feature expansive vistas, half-mile-long gravel bars and vast windrows of bleached snags. The flood plain is more than a mile wide in many places, and the river roams it during high water. Sometimes cherished slots and pools are filled overnight with gravel, or are abandoned by the river entirely. Drift boats and rafts are most common on these reaches, and the names of the Hoh boat ramps and campgrounds are evocative of the very essence of Olympic Peninsula winter steelhead fly-fishing. During the early season, when the Hoh Tribe's hatchery fish return to the lower river, anglers speak of Barlow's Bar, Nolan Creek, G & L Shake, Cottonwood, Allen's Bar and the Oxbow. Later, as wild fish become the main show, the action often shifts upstream, to Willougby Creek, Minnie Peterson, Morgan's Crossing, Spruce Creek and the park ramp.

"A lot of people like the Hoh because its easier to wade and easier to fish than the Sol Duc or other Quillayute rivers," Dave Steinbaugh said. "It's also easier boating. It's more Skagit style where you cast and swing. A lot of people from those areas are more comfortable on it. It's such a beautiful place. The place you fish depends on the condition of the water. When it's too gray down low, sometimes you need to go upstream."

If you go upstream far enough, you will enter the national park. The only boat ramp in the park is a short distance upstream from the entrance, and you almost never see boats above it. Steelhead are also less abundant than downstream, and they are more spread out, but there are usually enough to make it worth your time, and a couple of years ago Olympic National Park set aside approximately six miles of water between the boat ramp and one-quarter mile downstream of the campground as year-round, fly-only, catch-and-release water. Large portions of the fly water are braided, meandering riffles, but there is also clearly identifiable holding water. All the fish that the Huelsdonk girls caught a couple of miles downstream still return to the park, along with spring and fall chinook, coho salmon, anadromous and resident char, and summer and winter steelhead.

"As the Sol Duc gets too low and clear rivers like the Hoh and Queets become more fishable," J.D. Love said. "I generally use the same kinds of lines, even on the Hoh and Queets. I've gone to 120- to 160-grain lines most of the time."

One of the nicest things about the park water is that it is usually at least a half-mile from the road, forcing you to hike through perhaps the world's most exquisite temperate zone rain forest. The light is filtered through the ambient green lens of the forest canopy, and the air has an exhilarating ozone quality. On your way to the river, you will see rows of huge trees in straight lines. They are called colonnades, and the trees got a head start as seedlings on a fallen nurse log. You will see trees on stilts. They began on top of long-forgotten stumps and spread their tap roots over it as they grew. There are big-leaf maple groves, dripping with moss and licorice fern, and closer to the river, stands of lichen-covered alders. The forest floor is spongy and more open than other forests, the result of year-round cropping by Roosevelt elk.

Usually, you have to wade a side channel or spring pool to reach the mainstem. Tributary streams also meander across old glacial terraces, sometimes seemingly encircling you. There are squishy swales, where enormous skunk cabbage grow in spring, and forested wetlands riven by elk tracks. All of this is all excellent juvenile-fish habitat. Steelhead overwinter in the creeks, occasionally even burying themselves in the gravel during high water. Cutthroat swim higher than the steelhead, while coho prefer the lower-gradient off-channel areas and ponds. In a region dominated by rainfall, the wetlands and flood-plain complex in the Hoh in Olympic National Park reign supreme.

"Ocean conditions give us the big peaks and troughs," said John McMillan, who was a fish biologist with the Hoh Tribe before signing on with the Wild Salmon Center. "But habitat is the bank account."

Chapter Eleven

Industrial-Strength Flies

The first couple of months of winter, when storm system after storm system slams into the West End and the rivers absorb up to 40 inches of rain, is not usually the best time of year to fish a Spey fly. This is when you need a fly that will cut through the water column quickly, and that will maintain its appeal despite the abuse of heavy currents and rocky bottoms. Some anglers still fish classic patterns like the Royal Coachman Bucktail. "I think there is something about the Bucktail Coachman," Dick Goin told me a while back. But in recent years most of the Olympic Peninsula fly-fishing guides have switched over to patterns that feature marabou and rabbit strips.

"You need a more industrial-strength fly for those conditions, especially when you are guiding clients," J.D. Love told me.

As a steelhead fly-tying material, marabou has been around at least since the 1930s, when Al Knudson created his White Marabou, but the widespread application of marabou didn't occur until the early 1980s, when Puget Sound fly-fishing guide John Farrar and Kaufmann's Streamborn manager, Bob Aid, developed the Marabou Spider. Steelhead Bunnies, which are essentially leech patterns, are the creations of California angler, Mel Kreiger. But rabbit-strip patterns, similarly, didn't become standard in the Northwest until Farrar and the Kaufmann's crew began experimenting with them. The introduction of synthetic materials, especially those that created flash and sparkle, coincided with the development of marabou and rabbit-strip patterns, and they are widely used to enhance their fish appeal today.

The features that have propelled these flies to the foreground of winter steelhead patterns, that have, in effect, made them the currency of the realm throughout the Northwest, are easy to understand. The materials are cheap, they are widely available and come in the entire spectrum of colors. They are also easy to work with. Marabou, in particular, is extremely mobile, while rabbit is durable. As with Spey flies, spiders and leeches create a large profile without the burden of an excess of buoyant materials. In terms of fly design, they also, however unintentionally, finally liberated steelhead flies from the "insect" profile that had been in place for more than a century.

"In the last 10 to 15 years, fly tying has gotten so much freer," Skip Morris told me one afternoon as we discussed flies in his Port Ludlow home. The author of more than a dozen books on fly-tying and fly-fishing, Skip is widely heralded for his skill as both a fly-tier and fly-designer. "Anything goes these days. It's affected all types of fly-tying. For example if you look at *Art Flick's Streamside Guide* you will see that all those flies are almost exactly the same form. All of the steelhead flies I remember seeing as a kid, the flies in Enos Bradner's *Northwest Angler* and Bergman's *Trout*, were very close in form. Even when I was tying flies for Kaufmann's early in the 1980s, they all had pretty much the same form."

Skip believes the new materials have been partly responsible for the transformation in steelhead-fly design. "Marabou has really moved into fly-tying," he said. "It's fairly durable and so soft. If the fly jiggles the least bit, it sends a wave down the fly. You don't get that with a bucktail. As a material, it's so much more supple and responsive."

Skip also credits input from guides in the creation of the new generation of winter steelhead flies. "I think a lot of what happens to fly patterns comes from guides and people who fish a lot," he said. "They want things pragmatic, that you can tie and fish quickly and easily. I think that people who don't fish very often but tie a lot tend to come up with the most complicated and ornate flies. There is nothing wrong with that. There are guys who would rather tie than fish. But guides have a combination of a lot of experience on the water and are usually competent fly tiers. They have a good sense of things that will work. You get a lot of the bizarre looking flies that work and are usually easy to tie from guides."

I wouldn't use the word bizarre to describe the fly that J.D. Love showed Jay Brevik and me one early winter afternoon, but it was certainly unusual. Jay and I had stopped by J.D's house on the way home from the upper Bogachiel. Jay is a commercial fishermen, and he wanted to thank J.D. for an earlier trip by dropping off several frozen black cod rounds. J.D. lives on the Sol Duc, and we intercepted him walking back from the river. With his Spey rod slung over his shoulder and his dog, a high-spirited Dratthaar that he hunts above the Grande Ronde for chukars, J.D. looked like the living inspiration for a painting by his friend, celebrated fish and wildlife artist, Jack Datisman.

When we got out of the truck, Jay noticed the large flowing fly in the keeper ring of J.D.'s rod. "What kind of fly is that?" he asked.

J.D. removed the fly and held it up for us to inspect. "It's a shank fly," he said.

It was about five inches long. Most of its length was accounted for by a number of long ostrich strips that had been dyed a deep purple. Long, spiky black hackle had been palmered up the body, and black marabou was tied in behind the head. Touches of flash, a soft pale blue like the flats off the Florida Keys, had been added with Krystal Flash. In combination, these materials created a stunning, leggy, prawn-like fly, but that wasn't the unusual part; the thing that set it apart was that it wasn't tied on a hook.

"Is it a tube fly?" I asked.

"No, it's not tied on a tube," J.D. said. "It's tied on a shank, a Waddington shank."

J.D. parted the hackle and revealed something that looked like a bobby pin. It had a downturned eye and a second loop at the tail end of the fly that was parallel to the ground. "You run the leader through the eye, then down the top of the shank." J.D. pulled a plastic sleeve off the back of the shank. "The leader goes through the back loop and then you tie on the hook." He slipped the sleeve back over the end of the shank to keep the hook in place.

"Does it work?" I asked.

J.D. smiled. "I wouldn't use it if it didn't," he said.

We talked about the fly a little more, then the topic switched to bird dogs. But the shank fly intrigued me, and when I visited J.D. at his riverside fly-tying cabin a few months later I brought it up again.

"Did you invent the shank fly?" I asked.

He shook his head. "Dave Steinbaugh and I came up with them as steelhead flies more or less independently," he said. "But other people have had the same concept." To make his point, J.D. found a Japanese fly-fishing catalogue and showed me flies very similar to his. He also pointed out Atlantic salmon patterns tied on shanks.

It is pretty easy to see the attractions of shank flies. Like Spey flies, they present a large profile, a very large one in the case of J.D.'s purple fly. Yet the marabou and hackle are more durable, easier to find and cheaper than many of the materials, even replacement materials, used in Glasso patterns. Because they can be tied in as many colors as you can imagine, they can be fished throughout a range of conditions—darks in turbid water, pinks in cold and clear water, and reds in water with color. The small hook, often simply an egg hook or beak hook, also makes it easier to hold fish than the larger hooks on standard marabou and rabbit dressings. They also sink well, an important consideration in early winter flows. All of these qualities combine to make shank flies one of the more important innovations in steelhead fly design in years.

Which brings me back to Skip Morris' dining room, a short time after we had eaten the stir fry that Skip had prepared for lunch.

"Steelhead flies mainly fall into the category of attractor patterns," he continued "That's partly why you can get pretty abstract with them. They aren't trying to imitate anything. The trend is toward more limits being explored more deeply. But at the same time I am constantly amazed at how picky fish can get at flies that don't imitate anything. Despite the illogic of it, I have found that the design in attractor flies can be critical. That is a sentence that sounds real illogical when you first say it. But, boy, I have seen plenty of times when it had to be the right design or it didn't work."

Perhaps part of the reason J.D. and Dave's shank flies are so productive is that they actually do imitate something. With their trailing tendrils of goose and pulsing marabou and rabbit bodies, these flies may be quite suggestive of one of the staples of a steelhead's diet at sea—squid. Indeed, squid and fish account for upwards of 90 percent of a steelhead's diet once it leaves the continental shelf for the open ocean. It seems reasonable that the steelhead returning to the rivers of the West End of the Olympic Peninsula—which includes fish that stay at sea longer than any other race of winter steelhead—would respond to a fly that suggests a squid. On the west side of Whidbey Island, after all, non-fly anglers do very well casting "hoochies," which are plastic salmon trolling lures that represent squid, into the surf for migrating winter steelhead.

I recently asked Jim Kerr, proprietor of The Port Townsend Angler, if he used shank flies. "I like them," he said. "But I've been too busy to tie very many flies this winter. I've just been fishing rabbit strips, mostly in white." He laughed. "I've just been tying them on the hook with an overhand knot."

That is really an industrial-strength fly.

Chapter Twelve

The Creeks

The Port Townsend Angler is Jefferson County's only fly shop, and I tend to stop by when I am in town. I usually need some tippet material or a pheasant feather or something. It's a small shop but it's got pretty much everything you need. It's also nice to talk to Jim Kerr or Joe Crecca, the shop's co-owners, about how they have been doing and where the fish are biting. We talk about the fishing that is the focus of their guiding operation—saltwater fishing for sea-run cutthroat or West End steelhead. Several years ago, Jim and Joe used a funky pickup canopy at the Three Rivers Resort, near the confluence of the Bogachiel and Sol Duc rivers, as their base of guiding. That's the sort of thing people in their twenties do.

Recently, I learned something about Jim that I hadn't known before.

"Do you ever fish creeks?" I asked absently, as I fingered the little bins of sea-run cutthroat patterns.

Jim's eyed twinkled, as they have a tendency to do when he's going to tell you something that you don't expect to hear. "Oh, yeah," he said. "I fish creeks. I love creeks."

The "creeks" we were talking about are the relatively short-run, cedar-stained streams that drain the foothills of the Olympic Peninsula. They are easy to pick out on a map because they head up outside the mountainous core of the Olympics. Every corner of the peninsula has brushy, low-gradient creeks—Chimacum Creek in the Olympic rainshadow, Lilliwaup Creek on Hood Canal and MacDonald Creek near Sequim. Most of them support anadromous fish, usually chum and coho salmon, sea-run cutthroat and winter steelhead. But the West End is the only place you can still legally fish creeks for steelhead.

"Do you fish your Spey rod?" I asked.

"Nah," he said. "I just fish a single-handed rod. I use a floating line and about a 12-foot leader and a split shot about this far up the leader." He held his hands about 18 inches apart.

We talked about specific rivers for a few moments, about the Pysht and Hoko, the Sooes and Goodman Creek. Then the conversation drifted to tackle and strategies.

"Egg patterns?" I asked.

"Some," he said. "And a lot of Popsicles."

The Lyre River is the first stream west of the Elwha that is open during the winter steelhead season. Although it only drains about four miles on its journey from Lake Crescent to the Strait of Juan de Fuca, the Lyre doesn't have the feel of a creek, and its nickname—"the ditch"—pretty much describes its fly-fishing potential. But as you continue west, toward the northwest tip of the state at Neah Bay, you climb up and down one spur after another. On clear days, there are wonderful views of the strait and Vancouver Island from the crests, and there is a creek at the bottom of every rise. East and West Twin rivers come first, then Deep Creek, and then the Pysht, Clallam, Hoko and Sekiu. Heading south from Cape Flattery, the rivers that flow into the ocean all have their mouths on either Indian reservations or Olympic National Park. But the Makah Tribe will sell you a permit to fish the Sooes Rivers, and there is road access to at least small portions of the Ozette River and Goodman, Mosquito, Kalaloch and Cedar creeks.

Before Euro-American settlement in the 1850s, the small rivers and creeks of the western strait and north coast were extremely productive anadromous fish systems. Rising up on foothills that reached up to 3,000 feet, the rivers chattered downstream over 10- to 15-mile watercourses. The abundance of old-growth blowdown within the channels slowed their descents and created staircase-like pathways for migrating fish. In the lower-gradient downstream reaches, networks of huge log jams slowed the rivers even further, and the tides reached several miles upstream. There were deep pools, filled with clean gravel. The creeks ran clear nearly year round, and the dense overstory of old-growth Sitka spruce, hemlock and cedar kept them cool in summer. The maze of off-channel areas were superb juvenile rearing habitat for steelhead, cutthroat and coho salmon, while the estuaries were heavily used by chum and chinook salmon.

"A small group of us fished the Pysht and other Strait of Juan de Fuca streams back in the fifties," Dick Goin recalled. "I had a '29 Model A. It was very common for us to have to pull a tire off and patch it or to slap chains on. The Pysht closed at Burnt Mountain Road then and the Hoko closed at the Iron Bridge. The Hoko wasn't as good as the Pysht but it had a different class of fish—bigger ones, to 20 pounds. It wasn't unusual to hook 10 or 12 fish a day either, but we got tore out a lot." According to Dick, they usually quit fishing before the end of the season. "By the 10th or 12th or 15th of February, it was really common to hook kelts," he said. "We wanted no truck with them."

Unfortunately, none of the West End steelhead and salmon rivers have been as badly served by their corporate and government stewards as the creeks. Logging is the most visible habitat-degrading activity in the northwest corner of the peninsula, of course, and since none of the creeks enjoy headwater protection within Olympic National Park, they have typically been harvested from ridgeline to tidewater. Today, the creeks drop quickly from the slopes, unfettered by large timber, and they flow through corridors of young alder. Pools and spawning gravel have declined. Salmon and trout redds choke beneath sediment or are destroyed by scour. Chinook have virtually disappeared, and there are currently no in-river fisheries for any salmon species. Wild steelhead populations have declined significantly.

The Reagan-era liquidation of more than 5,000 acres of old growth in the headwaters of the Pysht River to finance a leveraged stock buy out probably takes the prize for sheer timber industry arrogance. But in terms of its affect on fisheries nothing approaches the devastation that occurred on Deep Creek. A small system, draining only 17 square miles, Deep Creek was, nonetheless, noted for its salmon and steelhead, and it was the historic site of a year-round S'Klallam village. Extensive clear-cut logging and road building on steep U.S. Forest Service holdings began in the 1970s, and over the next 20 years, 134 separate landslides were documented. They culminated in November of 1990, when a huge slide was set in motion by road failures below clear cuts on Forest Service land. The slide gathered an enormous amount of mud, rock and water as it tore downstream. It downcut as much as 10 feet into the stream bed and scoured the creek from river mile 12 down to river mile 2. It is also suspected of triggering a 10-acre collapse into the lower river that deposited thousands of cubic yards of sediment.

Timber harvest is far from the only factor at play in the decline of the creeks, of course, and in recent years timber practices have improved markedly, especially on the Merrill-Ring Tree Farm on the lower end of the Pysht drainage. The late Buck Adamire logged the West End for nearly a half-century and was widely known for going out of his way to follow timber practices that protect fish and wildlife habitat. While acknowledging that there were logging abuses in the past and that they had an effect on individual fish runs, he didn't believe they were the major factor in the salmon and steelhead's collapse. Like many long-time Olympic Peninsula residents, he attributed that to overharvest, both sport and commercial. With decades of experience in the woods, he also had a unique perspective on the way rivers like the Hoko, Pysht, Sekiu and Ozette were historically managed by state agencies.

"The Hoko River is one of my favorite streams," he wrote me several years ago. "Seems anymore compared to the past, it just looks like it's about to rain and the river is muddy right now or immediately. About nine miles upstream from Highway 112, the river is eroding a stretch of clay bank causing slides, but Crown Pacific has so many new logging roads on (the) east side lower river that has to be a factor too. The Hoko contains some of the best or superb spawning gravel of any area stream. Fisheries blew out a portion of two river falls in 1970s to improve fish passage."

Buck was the boss at the last live-in log camp on the Olympic Peninsula. "During the early 1970s, I was foreman at ITT-Rayonier's live-in Hoko River Camp," he wrote. "I was given a legal description and maps of all timber tracts scheduled for logging for three years. I also was given a list of streams marked with N.I. or F.I., meaning "fisheries not interested" or "fisheries interested." The classifications were the result of stream surveys conducted during the summer, and many were identified as not bearing fish.

"My first fall during late November I was showing my assistant where next to move a machine, as I was taking time off due," he said. "There was felled and bucked timber all over this flat tract, including a stream. Hearing much water splashing, I investigated.

There were at least a dozen salmon, some of which were spawning, where we had a green light to log across said stream." Buck pursued the matter, and the company ordered its environmental forester to inspect the site. "He ordered no logging until June 1, and personally oversaw cleaning of the stream which we didn't really have to do.

"...I wonder how many streams elsewhere were logged regardless of fish because fisheries had underclassified certain streams?"

Additionally, the mouths of many rivers, including the Pysht and Hoko, have been dredged, and rivers have been the site of log drives. Many creeks and estuaries have been cleaned of woody debris, as well. For chinook and chum salmon, especially, the degradation of estuaries has a profound negative effect on their productivity. But sea-run cutthroat also make extensive use of estuaries, and steelhead at least need river mouths that are not blocked, as the Clallam River is on occasion, or have become so clogged with gravel that they become a maze of braided channels. This accumulation of sediment and gravel at river mouths usually occurs after dredging and diking, which are done, ostensibly, to reduce flooding. In reality, these actions often restrict the tidal reach in the lower river, and that reduces the ability of the river and tides to transport sediment out to sea. As a result, gravel builds up and flooding is actually more frequent.

Today, the WDFW probably poses more of a threat to the steelhead in creeks than the timber industry. It eventually closed all fishing on Deep Creek after the slides. Despite the fact that spawning escapements were not regularly monitored on any Strait of Juan de Fuca creeks until the mid-1980s and that the tribes do not accept the state's escapement targets on these rivers, the agency has unilaterally characterized Pysht and Hoko wild winter steelhead as "healthy" and allows wild harvest. Conceding that it has no idea of the status of the remaining Strait of Juan de Fuca or coastal creeks, the agency requires wild release on the West Twin, Clallam and Sekiu rivers. It also closes the season at the end of February on all creeks except the Hoko, apparently to protect late-returning wild fish. But hundreds of the much rarer early-timed wild steelhead have been killed on the Pysht and Hoko in recent years. Moreover, Big River, a tributary to Lake Ozette, and Goodman, Mosquito, Cedar and Kalaloch creeks—rivers about which virtually nothing is known—remain open to wild harvest.

If this seems insane, consider a conversation I had a few years ago with one of the WDFW fish division managers. I expressed concern about the increased pressure on the region's small systems and wondered if wild release should be implemented. "We use catch-and-release when runs aren't healthy," he sniffed with irritation, "not when they are." In other words, unless you can prove that the runs are unhealthy, they remain open to wild harvest. "No data, no problem" is the way I have heard this concept described. More recently, I mentioned to a different manager that Olympic National Park now prohibits wild harvest on its share of the Ozette, Mosquito, Cedar and Kalaloch creeks. "Yeah," he said contemptuously. "They like to pretend they are managing in the mid-19th century."

A while back, Dick Goin and I spent time talking about small streams, and he mentioned that the WDFW had proposed reopening Deep Creek for steelhead fishing.

"What?" I said, not sure that I had heard him right.

I had heard him right, and in 2002 the Washington Fish and Wildlife Commission adopted the recommendation. The Point No Point Treaty Council tribes objected strenuously to reopening the river before the Commission vote, and continued its objections after it was implemented. WDFW biologists insist that Deep Creek has reached its escapement goals in recent years—the goals the tribes dispute—and can support a catch-and-release fishery directed at its wild steelhead.

"What's the justification for opening Deep Creek?" I asked Dick.

He snorted, disgustedly. "What's the justification for opening Deep Creek? Well, officially, I imagine they'd say that it's to give fishermen more opportunity. In reality, it is just a justification for giving all of the major rivers over to the guides. In the East Twin we know that virtually all of the fishermen were crooks (who killed wild fish despite the regulations). There was intense pressure to reopen Deep Creek. There will be no enforcement. Why have 25 or 30 crooks when you can have two or three?"

Long-time Elwha S'Klallam tribal fisheries biologist, Michael McHenry, who has worked for years in the Deep Creek basin and was one of the authors of its restoration plan, outlined some of his objections to the fishery in a private letter to the Commission:

* "There's no harvestable surplus of steelhead in Deep Creek as total escapement to the basin is less than 400-500 fish." (surveys between '94 and '01 indicated escapement ranged between 117 and 211 steelhead).

* "Deep Creek is not and has not been planted with Chambers Creek fish since the 1980s; therefore, the relatively low numbers of wild fish could be proportionally more impacted by mortality from hooking and poaching.

* "Deep Creek, although already closed, has a serious poaching problem and enforcement is virtually non-existent on Olympic Peninsula rivers. This problem can only be expected to increase if Deep Creek is open to angling."

" . . . it is apparent to me that Deep Creek should not be opened to any kind of harvest pressure at this time," Mike concluded. "Indeed, an adjacent watershed, the East Twin River, was recently closed to steelhead harvest for many of the reasons cited above (while ironically the West Twin remains open despite very similar steelhead populations). I suspect Deep Creek is being offered as a sacrifice to make up for that perceived "loss of angling opportunity." This is a rather sad commentary on what really drives management decisions concerning steelhead in Washington."

So what is a fly-fisher to do in the face of such institutional intransigence? Well, the best antidote I know is to throw an 8-weight in a car and head for a creek. During early winter, there are usually plenty of hatchery fish around, and they aren't that difficult to catch. Indeed, there is probably no better place to hook your fish winter steelhead on the fly than a small cedar creek.

"I just hike up as high as I can, then work my way back down," Jim Kerr said. "I roll cast to one bank, then the other. I swing the flies. The fish are in the slots and behind the little rocks, any little bit of cover. If you can get in before the gear guys, you can have a great time. You'd be surprised how many fish there are. If you want to fly-fish and keep a couple of fish to eat, that's the way to do it."

But leave Deep Creek steelhead alone.

Chapter Thirteen
The Big Rod

It took me a lot longer to become comfortable with a Spey rod than most of my friends. I first became aware of two-handed rods on West End rivers during the 1980s, and by the beginning of the 1990s the fly-fishing guides fished them nearly exclusively during the winter. But I didn't have any first hand contact with Spey casting until I floated the middle Sol Duc with Bob Pigott and his daughter Erin about 10 years ago. Bob rowed most of the day, but he occasionally anchored and fished. I was, not surprisingly, impressed by the great ellipses of fly line that he shot, seemingly effortlessly. I also saw the great advantage the long rod had for mending and line control. At one point, we pulled onto a sand bar and Bob gave me a brief lesson in the basic Spey cast. I understood immediately that the long Celtic rod was the perfect implement for the big steelhead and the large rivers of the West End.

Two-handed rods, of course, are far from recent innovations. They were developed during the 19th century on Scotland's Spey River, the same fertile ground where Spey flies originated and where heavy brush and high banks made traditional backcasts difficult. The great English expatriate fly-fisher, General Noel Money, introduced two-handed rods for steelhead on Vancouver Island's Stamp and Little Qualicum rivers in the 1920s. As dressings for winter steelhead emerged, Vancouver Island's other great fly-fishing pioneer, Roderick Haig-Brown, identified another advantage of the two-handed rod. "A sensible man, fishing a large fly in a river like the Campbell," he wrote in his 1939 volume *The Western Angler*, "would use a twelve- or thirteen-foot double-handed rod. It is easier, more comfortable and less tiring than fishing a single-handed rod heavy enough to cast a 2/0 fly." But Spey rods, unaccountably, didn't become popular south of the 48th parallel until really large flies and heavy sink-tips were introduced more than 50 years later.

Although I fell under the thrall of the Spey rod instantly, it took me a few years to assemble the complete outfit, largely because they are expensive. During that time, they became increasingly common on West End rivers, and it almost reached the point that you were no longer taken seriously as a winter steelheader unless you fished a two-handed rod. I continued fishing with my 8-weight single-handed rod, and I had about the same level of success as always. But I had managed to convince myself that every difficulty that had ever deviled me as a winter steelheader would simply vanish once I got my Spey rod. I am not usually anywhere near this susceptible to the entreaties of new fishing technology, but that was exactly the point: Spey rods aren't new. They have been around for more than 100 years, and have proven themselves on two continents and on two of the greatest sport-fish species that ever swam.

"Spey rods are good for a number of reasons," Dave Steinbaugh told me when I asked him for advice about the type of rod I should select. Dave is a master with the two-handed rod and regularly conducts Spey-casting clinics at his shop Waters West Fly Fishing Outfitters in Port Angeles. "They are an efficient use of your energy. The fly is fishing more time during the day because it is in the water longer. You can also cover at least double the amount of water. Control of the line and the fly is incredible. Plus they are a lot of fun. Actually, distance is one of the least important things about the Spey rod, even in winter. It's fun to boom your line out there, but most people forget that the fish are right in front of them." As for the actual rod, Dave prefers a more traditional, softer action on a Spey rod. "I like a stiffer action on a single-handed rod but prefer a more traditional Spey action on a two-handed rod. I like 14- or 15-footers for winter fish."

After all my anticipation, it probably shouldn't have surprised me that my first experience with the big rod turned out considerably less grand than I had imagined. I had played around with my 14-foot rod in the yard a couple of times, but the casting instruction pamphlet advised that you needed to be on the water to properly load the line. I had also seemed to pick up the basic stroke fairly well when Bob Pigott had showed it to me years before. So I got in the car and headed to the Sol Duc. I did all right on relatively short roll casts with a floating line, and I loved the long rod's mending reach, but things began to unravel quickly when I switched over to the 15-foot sink-tip. It was harder to roll cast, and when I tried to perform an actual Spey cast the line collapsed like a mallard with two broken wings. I couldn't seem to recall what either Bob or Dave had told me. I ended up spending most of the day fishing the rod like, well, like a very expensive cane pole.

Believe it or not, that pattern pretty much repeated itself for the next two winters. I studied the casting pamphlet a number of times, but I am a hopelessly verbal person, and I seem congenitally incapable of learning anything from diagrams. Since most instructional literature tends to be assembled by people whose expertise is in performing the task, not in language, the written manuals also tend to be more confusing than illuminating, at least for me. I should have sent away for one of the Spey-casting videos. I also should have simply driven over to Waters West and signed up for a clinic, but I was an outdoor writer, damnit, and I didn't want to appear as awkward, stupid or embarrassed as I felt. So I spent the better part of two winters fishing my Spey rod until it drove me crazy, then switching to the 8-weight when I really wanted to fish.

The nadir of this self-mortification with the Spey rod occurred on a trip to the Hoh with Larry Dennison. Larry is a veteran Olympic Peninsula fly-fisher and former Jefferson County Commissioner. During his tenure, he accomplished a lot of good things, including saving my favorite lake, Gibbs Lake, from development, but he is best remembered for chairing a meeting on the summit of Mount Olympus. Larry and I had donated a free fishing trip to raise funds for the Washington Environmental Council, and we decided to indulge ourselves in a "scouting" expedition before guiding the person who won the trip. In a gesture of forcing myself to deal with the Spey rod, I left my single-handed road at home. But I hadn't fished the two-hander in nearly a year, and I had a terrible time that day. It was all I could do to keep from throwing the whole kit and caboodle into the river. Hell, I felt like throwing myself into the river. I began to wonder if, at 50 years of age, I had simply passed the point where I would ever be able to learn anything new again.

It didn't help matters any when late in the afternoon Larry and I switched rods. He had only ever handled a Spey rod once, at a clinic Jim Kerr of the Port Townsend Angler had put on, but he had a much better feel for it than I did.

Fortunately, on our way back from the Hoh, Larry and I swung off 101 and drove a few miles to one of our favorite drifts on the upper Sol Duc. It isn't one of the widely known locations for out-of-town or casual anglers, so we were a little surprised to see a vehicle parked at the end of the two track. Even more surprising, the old blue pickup with the small camper canopy had Alberta plates, the ones that say "Wild Rose Country."

"We don't see those around here very often," Larry said.

"I wonder if they're fishing?" I asked, and, sure enough, when we peeked in the back of the canopy we could see several rod tubes.

We hiked the short distance to the river, and Larry waded into the soft water at the head of a long section of pocket water. I splashed through the shallows downstream to an exposed bar where I could fish the slicks and boulders above a rapids. I removed the Type III sink-tip from my loop system, and attached a 15-foot floating line. With the dry line, I was at least able to flip out a decent roll cast. I fished a black General Practitioner on a long leader. It was the first fun I had had all day.

After I reached the edge of the rapids, I decided to wade back upstream and fish the same water again with a different fly. When I turned around, I saw a fisherman walking down the bank toward the river. He was an older man, quite tall and thin. There was a hitch in his gate, and he leaned on a walking stick. As we drew closer, I noticed that he was carrying a Spey rod. His tackle was of excellent quality, but, even better, it had the look of having been used hard and well tended.

"Another fly-fisherman," he said, with a craggy smile.

"Oh yeah," I said. "There are quite a few around here these days."

"You're the first one I've seen all week," he said. There was a Scandinavian lilt to his speech. "Have you been doing any good?"

I shook my head. "How about you?"

"This is my first time here. I've just been poking around looking at things. You have some lovely rivers."

"You fish a Spey rod, I see?"

He nodded, smiling. "You too. They're good, eh?"

"Well, I'm not any good at it yet. I can't seem to get the hang of it."

He smiled again. "You've probably been fishing a long time."

I nodded.

"It was hard for me too," he said. "You've got to learn not to push it so hard. But you've just got to stay with it. I was always putting it away and using my one-handed rod. I didn't get better until I decided that was the only way I was going to fish."

We talked a while longer, about the Thompson, his home water, and the Gold and Skeena. I told him how to get to a couple of good places for fly-fishing on the lower river. Then he waded into the water, leaning on his walking stick as he picked his way through the rocky shallows. He seemed awkward and sort of creaky wading, but when he took up position along the edge of the deep water, he was transformed. He stripped a few coils of line, tipped the rod back and roll cast to extend line. Then he brought the rod up over his shoulder, whipped it around and shot a long ribbon of line. It was fluid, elegant and seemingly effortless.

A couple of weeks later, I drove out to the Sol Duc by myself. The encounter with the old Canadian had rekindled my initial passion for the Spey rod. I didn't have a lot of time that day, so I picked one of the first places I could legally fish, a drift up near the deadline that Jay Brevik had showed me. It's the sort of broken-up pocket water the Sol Duc is famous for, and it was even thinner than usual this day. I attached a 15-foot floating tip and tied a mahogany and black Marabou spider onto my five-foot leader.

Remembering Dave's advice about not having to boom the line out, I stayed on the bank and flipped a few short roll casts along the inside current seam. Then I climbed over a couple of blow-down alders and waded to the head of the run. I stripped about twenty more feet of running line, roll cast, then flipped the line out into the middle of the current. When the line began to hang downstream, I brought the rod up over my shoulder, paused briefly as the line tagged the water, then cast. I knew from the way the rod felt that everything had gone well for once. And sure enough, the line in my left hand shot through the guides.

I was so thrilled about making a decent cast that I simply stood there for a few moments, letting the fly hang in the current. That was when the steelhead hit. A bright hen of about 10 pounds, it rapped the fly hard, then exploded into the air. It threw the barb-lesss hook on its third jump, as I was still trying to gather slack.

I was far from unhappy, though. “Okay,” I said, out loud. “Okay. That’s better.”

Chapter Fourteen

Sol Duc

In a region where fly-fishers have historically been as rare as albino crows, the Sol Duc River has gradually become hallowed ground for Olympic Peninsula fly-anglers with a sense of tradition. The riffle a short distance of its confluence with the Bogachiel was Syd Glasso's favorite fly water, and his storied 18-pound, 12-ounce 1959 *Field & Stream* fishing contest winner was a Sol Duc steelhead. "Sol Duc" was the name Glasso gave one of his revolutionary series of Spey flies, which included the Sol Duc, and Sol Duc Spey. Later on, Jim Garrett developed exquisite steelhead and salmon flies when he lived at Bear Springs on the upper river. The Sol Duc was also the site of the first attempts to curtail the Chambers Creek hatchery plants, and it was where Bob Pigott, Herb Jacobsen, J.D. Love and other anglers obtained the first selective fishery, wild-release regulations for winter steelhead in the Quillayute System.

"It has a large run of native steelhead," J.D. Love said. "It's clear most of the time, sometimes too clear. The rocks make it hard to fish and there are fewer sections of classic fly water. But there is plenty of good swinging water if you look for it. Another thing about the Sol Duc is that it has steelhead almost all of the time. There are also beautiful cutthroat most of the time and salmon almost all year. I also think the Sol Duc has every bit as productive of insect hatches as the Gallatin and other famous Yellowstone-area freestone streams."

With a drainage of more than 219 square miles, nearly as much as the Bogachiel and Calawah combined, the Sol Duc is the largest Quillayute System river. It rises up on mile-high heather meadows and subalpine tarns near the head of the Hoh and Elwha rivers, then flows west between the North Fork of the Calawah and Strait of Juan de Fuca streams on its journey to the coast. Its complement of anadromous fish is the most varied of the

Quillayute rivers, including winter and summer steelhead, sea-run cutthroat, summer and fall chinook, as well as a unique stock of summer coho that returns to the river in August and early September, both lake- and river-dwelling sockeye, and a lake-dwelling strain of coho in Lake Pleasant. Its winter steelhead are arguably the healthiest stock in the region, and its fall chinook, fall coho and cutthroat stocks are also robust.

For fly-fishers from other parts of the country, or whose experience has been limited primarily to trout, the Sol Duc reveals itself more generously than the rainforest rivers, or even the Bogachiel. In its upper reaches especially, on the wild release water between the salmon hatchery at Sappho and the winter steelhead deadline at Snyder Creek, it features familiar riffle-pool-tailout sequences and pocket water, and potential steelhead holding water isn't hard to identify. Even the middle and lower river, which are swollen by Beaver, Lake, Schuwah and Gunderson creeks, contain familiar trout-stream architecture for the most part. The steelhead aren't always where you think they should be, but once you locate a fish the odds are excellent that the same spot will be productive for years to come.

The open visage of the Sol Duc is a result of its "bedrock-boulder confined" nature. That means that its river bed is comprised largely of rock, and that it tends to stays within its banks. Unlike on the glacial rivers, large trees grow to within a few feet of the channel, and the river clears and drops quickly even after heavy rain. Although this makes life easier for both anglers and spawning and juvenile fish, it is not without drawbacks. The recruitment of large woody debris is diminished compared to the more boisterous rivers to the south. However, Dick Goin has observed that large boulders have been remarkably stable on the Sol Duc over the last 50 years, and it is believed that they contribute the roughness and sinuosity that is normally the function of wood. The bedrock bottom holds heat better than gravel, though, and during summer it can result in higher water temperatures than salmonids prefer. Its dearth of wetlands is perhaps the Sol Duc's most troublesome natural feature, and human actions have exacerbated the problem.

"The state threatened condemnation proceedings where the Sol Duc Hatchery now stands," Buck Adamire informed me a few years ago. "My deceased friend Joe Pavel didn't want to sell. He tried to have (the) state just take say 5 to 10 acres where the spring enters the river but (the) state wanted it all. All that facility could have been consolidated on 5 to 10 acres. What a piece of property, surrounded by DNR land on a dead-end road and gradual sloping river bank, yet higher ground not subject to floods.

"A spring creek near the Sol Duc Bear Springs facility (satellite hatchery) where I once trapped beaver, otter and 'coons and which contained a small salmon run was straightened out like a ditch with a dam near the river. No fish ladder either. This spring creek was used for rearing purposes until they ran out of funds." Neither of these conversions of habitat is mentioned in the Washington Conservation Commission's Habitat Limiting Factors Analysis of the North Coast Streams.

Fly-fishers are not the only anglers who have heard of the Sol Duc, of course, and it is hit heavily by drift-boat anglers in its middle and lower reaches, basically from the hatchery downstream to the takeouts off the R3000 Road or at Leyendecker County Park, but there are ways to avoid the crowds.

"I like the Quillayute itself when the water is low enough to concentrate fish," Dave Steinbaugh told me. "I try to intercept them on an incoming tide. I also like to do that on the lower Sol Duc and Bogachiel. I try it two hours before or after the peak of the high tide. On the upper Sol Duc, I like the character of the holes. It is beautiful water with big holes. There is lot of water to fish around. It's fun to float down it, too."

Unless you are accomplished with a pair of oars, the upper Sol Duc is no place to launch a boat, though. It is much better to float it with someone who knows the river. The entire Sol Duc valley also has a reputation for poor bank-fishing access, and if you are driving around looking for a brown WDFW "Public Fishing" sign you won't see many, but a quick look at a map reveals a number of Forest Service and Department of Natural Resources holdings. There are also many areas of gated timber company land. Not all of these two-tracks and skid roads lead to good fishing, even fewer to good fly-fishing. But if you've got enough energy to prospect, you will find places to fish.

There are a few that you will remember on your death bed.

Chapter Fifteen

DEAD-DRIFT

It is a generally accepted notion out here that you can depend on a "midwinter thaw" some time in February. It doesn't always happen, and it certainly doesn't kick the thermometer up into anything that resembles the summer or even the late spring range, but there is usually a period of a week or so when the rain holds off and the temperature climbs up into the middle fifties. This is when the first blush of skunk cabbage brightens the alder bottoms and red-flowering currant appears up on the hillsides. It is also the time when many backpackers plan their first overnight of the new year, usually to the coastal strip in Olympic National Park.

Nearly 20 years ago, I took advantage of one of those breaks and drove out to Goodman Creek. I recall the weather clearly. It was 54 degrees when I passed through Forks, and the sky was blue, broken only by a few gauzy white clouds. The air had the sweet smell of awakening soil and burning slash. The Oil City Road was remarkably puddle free, and so was the Rayonier 3000 Road, the mainline between the Bogachiel and the Hoh. It felt good being on the road, on my first camping trip of the year.

I had two free days. In the past, I had hiked to the mouth of Goodman Creek along the beach, and I had fished a short distance above and below the Goodman Creek bridge on the mainline, but I had never gotten down near the national park boundary from the east. On this trip, I planned to hike downstream until I found a campsite far enough from the road that I wouldn't be bothered. I would fish around camp the first evening, then bushwhack down toward the park boundary in the morning. Old maps show a trail on the north side of the creek all the way to the mouth. I had never found any evidence of it around the bridge, but I thought I might connect with a remnant farther down. As is always the case with my schemes, the idea was to secure a stretch of river, pristine and unfished, all to myself.

I arrived at the bridge around two o'clock, slipped into my hip waders and retrieved my old green Kelty pack from the back of the truck. I intended to hike in the creek whenever possible, but knew there would be places I would have scramble out of the water, and the hip waders gave me more mobility than chest waders. It was tough-going in places, clambering above and under blow-down, skirting tangles of devil's club and wading around snags. I worked up a sweat quickly, but I was still in my early thirties and was having a good time. I hiked for about an hour, passed some nice-looking water, but left my rod in its tube. Eventually, I found a little glade beneath a couple of ancient, gnarled Sitka spruce. I set up the tent, stashed my gear inside, and headed back to the creek.

The alders on the south side of the stream were back-lit in brassy winter light, and I could tell from the sun's angle that I only had about an hour to fish. I threaded my floating line, tied a weighted hot pink egg pattern onto my tippet, waded into the riffle in front of my camp, then headed downstream. With the forest's streamers of moss and broken-off tree tops, it was easy to tell I was near the coast. I quickly came to a small pool. The head of it was cross-hatched with blowdown, but there was a sweet-looking tailout, free of obstruction, below it. I couldn't see more than a foot or so into the dark tannic water, but it looked like a great place for a steelhead to hold.

I got out of the water above the blowdown and scrambled along the bank until I was directly across from the pool. Easing cautiously back into the creek, I moved a few feet closer to the tailout. I cast upstream, toward the downstream edge of the alders. I tossed an upstream mend and followed the progress of the floating line with my rod. It drifted drag free along the outside edge of the tailout, then began to pick up speed as the bottom rose and the current quickened. I stripped in a couple of feet of line and flipped it back upstream. This time, my fly landed closer to midstream. I mended again and tracked it downstream.

The fish hit just as the fly came under tension and began to rise. It came out of the water immediately, writhing and twisting, then splashed back to the surface. It wasn't a big fish, only four or five pounds, but it was incandescent. In the gathering gloom of late afternoon, it looked like a light was shining on it. I was certain that it would slash upstream and break me off on the alders, but it didn't. It thrashed across the surface, kicking up spray, then blasted downstream into the next riffle. It fought its heart out for five minutes, but my leader was heavy. It was sort of like having a fist fight in a closet. When I finally brought it to hand, I was not surprised in the least that it was a wild fish.

That was the second winter steelhead I caught on a fly. I tended to concentrate on small streams and creeks in those days. The structure of small water was more comprehensible after years of fishing trout streams, and so was the tackle. All I really needed, after all, was a floating line, a leader the length of the rod, and an egg or nymph pattern. I had a sink-tip back then and had, in fact, hooked my first winter steelhead on it but I was more comfortable with the floater. That has changed over the years. Today, I spend most of my time on the larger rivers, and nearly always fish a sink-tip on a wet-fly swing. I still enjoy dead-drifting a fly on creeks and small streams, and many of my friends fish floating lines exclusively and do very well. Some fish the lines on a swing, especially on small water, but most fish their flies freely in the current, dead-drift.

"I always use a floating line these days," Dick Goin said. "That's all we had when I started fly-fishing. I couldn't afford the oil-finished or enameled lines. Then back in 1948, my friends and I began to make home-made shooting heads for trout fishing on Lake Mills. I also tried lead and full-sinking lines when they got better, and eventually sink-tips twenty years ago, but I finally thought 'The hell with it.' Since then, I've used a floating line and split shot if I need to get down. I've really enjoyed myself more. I've had a lot more fun.They can get down where I can't, but are they having fun?"

Dick has become so closely associated with this technique that it has been used to identify him. "I was fishing on the Hoh a while back," Dave Steinbaugh told me. "It was gloomy and raining and I saw a person fishing on the far side of the river. I couldn't tell who it was, but every time he cast I would see two splashes when the line hit the water. Then I realized it had to be Dick. One splash was for the fly and the other was for the split shot."

John McMillan hasn't been fishing a floating line on West End rivers as long as Dick Goin, but he comes by it naturally. The son of floating-line master and author of the steelhead fly-fishing classic, *Dry Line Steelhead*, Bill McMillan, John has fished a floating line since he was in grade school. "I average between 15 and 30 fish a winter on a dry line," he told me. John fishes large water with a Spey rod and throws a long line. "I am usually making 100- or 120-foot casts. I need that much line out so I can make the big mends to get the fly down."

The technique of fishing a fly dead-drift is straightforward: You cast up or across stream, mend the line to allow the fly to sink, and follow it downstream with the rod. If everything goes right, the fly will drift along near the bottom at the speed of the current. This is inherently different from the wet-fly swing, where the fly is cast across and downstream and worked across the face of the current. The point of both techniques is to give the steelhead a long, tantalizing look at the fly. A fly fished dead-drift is, at least theoretically, most effective when it is moving downstream, while the fly on a swing is, again theoretically, most likely to interest a fish when it is working diagonally or across the current. (In reality, hits often occur in both methods just as the fly begins to rise or change speed). Instead of relying on the weight of the line to carry the fly down, anglers fishing a floating line either add weight to the fly, fish a large fly or add split shot to the line. Long leaders, as long as 12 feet or more, and large upstream mends are often necessary in deep water.

It has often been pointed out that fishing a floating line for winter steelhead is virtually identical to nymph fishing for trout. Like nymph fishers, steelheaders typically concentrate on holding lies, usually cutbanks and snags along the bank, midriver shelves and slots, and tailouts. Rather than trying to cover a large area on a single cast, they concentrate on specific habit niches and fish them on as short a line as possible. Most of the time this involves taking up a position so you are facing the opposite bank and casting across the current, but on small streams, drifting your fly straight downstream on a slack line can be effective.

Right-angle nymphing is a recent refinement of dead-drift steelheading. The terminal tackle in this style of nymphing consists of a heavy section of monofilament attached to the floating line, a yarn strike indicator, and a leader that is the appropriate length for the depth you wish to fish. The butt end of your monofilament and strike indicator are heavily dressed with floatant, and the (undressed) leader is tied to the indicator at a 90-degree angle to the mainline and leader butt. In areas where the bottom contour is familiar, this technique allows for very precise control of the fly.

"It is very effective," said Chris Bellows, an avid winter steelhead fly-fisherman. "The thing I like about right-angle nymphing is that you don't have to be right on the bottom. Even on those cold January mornings, the steelhead would come up off the bottom for the fly. Another thing I like about nymphing is that the fly is not going to intimidate the fish. If they are there and they are aggressive, they'll hit it." Like John McMillan, Chris uses a Spey rod when he is fishing a floating line. "I might use a single-handed rod on some small creeks, but I usually fish my Spey rod" he said. "I pretty much just fished nymphs all winter last year. The only time it wasn't as productive was when there were too many boats."

Although weighted egg patterns, such as I used on Goodman Creek, are traditional when dead-drifting for winter steelhead, many different patterns are productive. I called Chris once when he was still working at Waters West and asked him to stash a selection of spring nymphs outside the shop so I could pick them up before he opened in the morning. His selection included not only eyed egg patterns, but also Bitch Creeks, Brindle Bugs, stonefly nymphs and an assortment of rubber-legged creations.

Although he ties them on 3/0 to 5/0 hooks so they will sink quickly on the big water he favors, John McMillan's flies are more traditional, as are the worn leather and sheep fleece fly wallets in which he stores them. John fishes a large version of his dad's Winter's Hope, a superb dead-drift fly in cold water, as well as General Practitioner variations in purples and orange, fuschia and black. John also fishes bead-head leeches with eyes that are tied on Waddington shanks, and a Glasso-inspired fly with a guinea. "I'm real picky with guinea," he said. "I usually only get about four feathers out of a box."

Whether you fish buggy patterns on creeks or large attractor patterns on glacial torrents, the important thing to remember about the floating line in winter is that it is most effective when it is fished to a specific holding area, rather than as a searching technique. This is true even when you have yards of line out.

"The big thing most people miss is the ability to locate their fly," Dick Goin said. "I very rarely fish a long drift. I've been a spot fisherman all of my life."

Chapter Sixteen
The Park

Jay Brevik and I were only about a mile from the road, but it felt like we had the entire upper Hoh to ourselves. It was February. The river was in great shape, low but with a trace of lime pulp green. A lot of winter steelhead had returned to the Hoh that year, and the boat ramps on the lower river were full of big trucks and boat trailers, but the only signs of life we had encountered all morning were elk and eagles. We had smelled elk as we hiked through the alder bottom near the road, and pre-mating eagles screeched and soared above the river. There were no wader prints on the sand bars, only old elk droppings and hoove prints.

It was our first trip to the upper Hoh since Olympic National Park had set aside a six-mile stretch of year-round "fly-only" catch-and-release water. A reach of braids and long riffles, it also contains good steelhead water if you are willing to look for it. Jay was working a waist-deep run between two washboard riffles. I had taken up position above a large snag and was hanging my fly along the edge of soft water behind it. We were both swinging big Marabou Spiders on sink-tips.

"There's a steelhead," Jay shouted, pointing downstream. "It's a nice one."

It was too far away for me to see. "That's a good sign," I said.

A few minutes later, Jay hollered again. "Jesus," he yelled.

I turned in his direction. He was backing up quickly and staring down at the water. "It bumped me," he said.

I didn't hear him correctly. "It bit you?"

"No, I don't think so," he said, still moving around and looking into the water. "It bumped into the back of my legs."

We stared at each other for a moment or two.

"Do you think it's trying to spawn or something?"

Jay shrugged. A half-smile came over his face. "It scared the hell out of me."

I started laughing. "I can imagine."

Whatever that steelhead's intent, we decided to leave it alone. Jay reeled his line in and waded back to the bank. We moved upstream a couple hundred yards.

A lot of people assume that Olympic National Park was created to protect the region's glacier-capped mountains, its unique temperate-zone rain forests and its wilderness beaches. The original impetus behind preserving a large tract of wilderness on the Olympic Peninsula was actually as a refuge for Roosevelt elk. The native elk of the coastal Northwest's dense rainy river valleys, Roosevelt elk had been extirpated from most of the Northwest by the late 19th century, and only around 2,000 were estimated to remain on the entire Olympic Peninsula. Elk were the reason President Theodore Roosevelt set aside 600,000 acres as the Mount Olympus National Monument in 1909, and when his cousin, President Franklin Roosevelt, signed the order designating Olympic National Park in 1938, the park was almost named "Elk National Park."

In the century since Teddy Roosevelt created an elk sanctuary in the central Olympics, the elk have responded to the protection. The park herd today numbers more than 5,000 elk and is the largest unmanaged Roosevelt elk population in the world. Moreover, it is widely acknowledged as the only genetically pure population of Roosevelt elk outside of Canada. All other coastal elk in Washington and Oregon are Rocky Mountain elk or contain Rocky Mountain elk genes today. They are the descendants of animals from Montana and Idaho and Wyoming that were released in the Northwest during the early 20th century to "restore" extirpated elk populations.

Fortunately, the umbrella of protection Olympic National Park provided the elk has also preserved many other species of native flora and fauna, even entire ecosystems. Some are internationally acclaimed—the upper reaches of the rainforest valleys, the glacial flanks of Mount Olympus and the 57 miles of wilderness seacoast. Others, such as the complex communities of epiphytes and mosses in the rainforest canopy, are much less widely known. Some of the strongest beneficiaries of the park's protection are the native salmonids of the rivers that drain the western slopes of the Olympic Mountains.

"The park is still a stronghold for wild steelhead and salmon," said John Meyer, Olympic National Park's chief fisheries biologist. "Our fall chinook and winter steelhead populations are some of the strongest in the region, although we have a few problems with coho. We don't have the largest size runs, but relative to their size they are very productive."

John and I spoke in his office near the ONP administration building in Port Angeles. A tall man with a fringe of white hair, John has the lean shape of someone who still spends time in a wet suit looking at fish. He is also an enthusiastic steelhead fisherman. During his 16 years at Olympic, John has been in the thick of the park's most contentious fish-management issues, including Elwha Dam removal, tribal salmon and steelhead allocation, and regulation changes for Lake Crescent's unique Beardslee and crescenti trout. I can't begin to remember how many meetings I have seen him at over the years. Through it all, he has remained knowledgeable and patient, often in the face of extreme provocation.

"We rely on the state and tribes for surveys, except for limited surveys on the Sol Duc and upper Bogachiel," he told me. "I have some concerns over the Sol Duc. The number of fish getting up into the park has been very variable. In the early 1990s, we saw a lot of steelhead up above the Salmon Cascades and around the hot springs, but the last few years it has really dropped down. We haven't seen many this spring either. They usually show up in late March and early April. They probably are just late this year, but it does seem to have declined and it does fluctuate a lot."

The park flies rafts into the upper Bogachiel near Flapjack, and the biologists float down to Undi Road, the road that connects Highway 101 with the Bogachiel River Trail. "There's substantial spawning up there," John said. "But I wish we had better information. The spawn timing seems earlier than I originally thought. It seems to start in early April. Also, some of our people have said that there is a fair amount of poaching going on up there and that they see people wading through redds."

The main reason migratory fish thrive in Olympic National Park, of course, is because of its high-quality habitat. Anyone who has ever spent any time hiking the upper reaches of these rivers can see first-hand the advantages that steelhead and salmon that spawn in the park have over fish that spawn downstream. The trees are larger, and when they fall down they remain in the river. There are complex, interconnected networks of habitat, ranging from side channels to springs to tributary mouths. The floodplains are intact, with cooling canopies of old-growth trees and immense log-jams. The spawning gravel is clean and stays in place throughout the winter.

"Habitat in the park is in pretty good shape," Meyer acknowledged. "We do see changes. We get natural catastrophes in the park. There was a big slide on the upper Hoh on Mount Tom Creek, but the slides that occur in the park are generally slowed down or stopped by the old-growth timber.

"I flew over two big slides on the upper Calawah a while back. One was on Sitkum Creek, outside the park, and the other was on the South Fork Calawah in a stand of old growth in the park. The slide outside the park began on a clear-cut ridge on a log road and went straight down hill, across the flood plain, and formed what looked like a dam. The river backed up, then cut through the dam. Sitkum Creek is still bleeding sediment into the mainstem.

"The whole hillside came down in the park, but it flowed into a tributary. The mass of rocks and trees stopped it. There was some sediment and turbidity for a few days, but it didn't carry down to the river."

Habitat isn't the only thing that separates the fish that spawn in the national park from those downstream, though. "We like to provide opportunity for fishermen," John said. "But conservation is our first priority."

Olympic National Park's fishing regulations pamphlet best illustrates the gulf between its approach to fish management and the state of Washington's. With the exception of rivers where harvest allocation issues with the tribes currently preclude catch-and-release, all park steelhead are now wild release. Selective fishery regulations, which prohibit bait or scents and restrict anglers to flies or artificial lures, have been implemented on the Bogachiel and upper Hoh, Queets and Quinault, as well as on the small steelhead rivers that are catch-and-release. In addition, the park requires wild release on the lower Queets during December and January to protect the wild early component of the run.

"The situation with early winter steelhead still bothers me," John said, as he stood up and removed a heavy volume from his bookshelf. "All of these rivers had substantial runs of early steelhead." Opening the book, he showed me a colored graph that began with a tall dominant peak on the left side of the page and then tapered rapidly to a series of progressively shallower peaks as it moved across the page to the right.

"That's a harvest graph of the Hoh," he said. He pointed to the tallest peak on the left. "Historically, the peak of the run on the Hoh occurred in December and January." Flipping pages, he also showed me graphs for the Queets and Quillayute System. They also peaked early in the season. "The peak of all wild steelhead was in January," he said. Then he moved his finger over to the lower series of peaks later in the season. "That's what were are catching now," he said. In other words, the largest component of the wild run today was the smallest part of it historically.

"The reason I'm concerned about the early steelhead is that early returning fish tend to go high in the system," he said. "If these fish were the ones spawning in the park, then we are missing these fish, and they are losing the best habitat we have left."

In recent years, no fish-management issue in the park has been more nettlesome than wild steelhead harvest on the Queets River. Although the park now requires wild release for nearly all native species, it still allows anglers to kill wild winter steelhead on the Queets between March 1 and April 15. Wild harvest on the Queets has been especially controversial because, after experimenting with more conservative management, the park actually increased harvest opportunity in the late 1990s. At the same time, the wild winter run size on the Queets has been in decline in recent years, and during the winters of both 2000 and 2001 the park imposed emergency early closures because of smaller than anticipated return.

"People call me up and ask, 'What in the hell is the park doing allowing wild fish to be killed?'" John explained.

According to John, the issue of wild-steelhead management on the Queets and other rivers traces back to unresolved harvest allocation issues with the tribes related to the Boldt Case. That is the 1974 federal court decision that ruled that western Washington treaty Indian tribes and non-tribal anglers were each entitled to 50 percent of the harvestable "surplus" of salmon and steelhead in a river. The Queets poses unique management problems, because although it flows entirely through Olympic National Park and the Quinault Indian Reservation, the state maintains an interest in the ability of non-tribal anglers to harvest their portion of its steelhead and salmon. Further complicating the matter, the tribe will not allow the National Park Service to participate in harvest negotiations between it and the state, and the WDFW and Tribe have never even agreed on a steelhead escapement target for the river.

"The National Park Service is within the Department of Interior," John said. "So is the Bureau of Indian Affairs. We have one set of attorneys. They work together and won't compete with each other when we have a legal issue."

John explained that the tribe has consistently harvested considerably more steelhead on the Queets than non-tribal fishermen, and several years ago the state of Washington filed suit in federal court in an attempt to equalize the fishery. "The Department of Interior attorneys called us and asked, 'Do you have an interest in this case?' We said we wanted our share of the fish to be caught or to spawn." But allowing a percentage of the park's steelhead to spawn, rather than be harvested, opened the specter of "foregone opportunity." Basically, foregone opportunity is the concept that if either party to the Boldt Decision intentionally does not harvest its share of the fish, the other group may claim it. The attorneys said, 'You can't do that. If you don't catch them, they (the tribes) can.'"

Foregone opportunity has never been challenged in court, but as John pointed out, the Department of Interior is not going to sue itself.

"We're trying to negotiate a new management approach," John said. "We'd like a harvest rate that is on a sliding scale. As the run size increases, the harvest rate increases. But the high end rates are still lower than MSH rates, and when you have lower runs it provides for more escapement."

John plans to retire shortly, and I am sure that he won't miss fielding phone calls about wild-steelhead harvest or attending meetings about the Elwha dams, but he looks back on his time at Olympic fondly. "It has been a dream come true," he told me. "I was always intrigued by the Olympics and I was thrilled to come out here. I was out on the South Fork of the Hoh a while back and I was thinking about what remarkable rivers these are."

He has a long-time goal of catching a steelhead from every Olympic Peninsula river, one he hasn't completed yet. "I'll still be going out there after I retire," he said.

Chapter Seventeen

Maximum Sustained Harvest

Doug Soule is a big guy, tall and broad shouldered, and I could see him above the throng of Christmas shoppers on Water Street in downtown Port Townsend. Doug was largely responsible for resurrecting the long-dormant East Jefferson County chapter of Trout Unlimited in the mid-1990s, and he has served as its president and most energetic activist. I knew he had almost certainly made it down to the Washington Fish and Wildlife Commission (Commission) meeting in Vancouver the previous weekend. One of the items on the agenda at the meeting had been the proposal, once again, to protect the remaining wild steelhead in Washington with mandatory wild release regulations.

"Hey, Doug," I hollered, and trotted across the street. "How did it go in Vancouver?"

"It looks good," he said. "There were a lot of people testifying for wild release. Way more than wanted to keep the harvest."

The effort to implement wild-steelhead release regulation on West End rivers has become as much a part of the Olympic Peninsula winter as recurring El Niños and mudslides. It became urgent after the winter of 2000, because, for all practical purposes, these rivers are now the last places in Washington where killing wild steelhead is still legal. Until recently, wild harvest was permitted on the Skagit, Stillaguamish and Snohomish rivers and many of their tributaries. But the wild runs on these systems collapsed to record low returns in the late 1990s, and the WDFW imposed emergency closures during 1999 and 2000, including closing even the popular March and April catch-and-release season. In early 2001, the Commission instituted permanent wild release regulations on all Puget Sound rivers except for the Seattle area's Green River. This points every angler who wants to kill a wild steelhead in one direction—the West End of the Olympic Peninsula.

"I suppose the King County Outdoor Sports Council was in favor of wild kill," I said.

Doug rolled his eyes. "There were these four old guys from Port Angeles that sat up front," he said. Doug said they were talking with WDFW steelhead managers opposed to wild release before the meeting. Then when it was their turn to speak, they basically repeated word for word the agency's argument against the proposal. "I said to a friend of mine, 'I can see that guy's lips moving but the words coming out are Gibbons'," Doug said.

"I know who they are," I said.

Unfortunately, the old cranks at the meeting have powerful and determined allies. Robert Gibbons, the lead author of the state's "Methodology for Determining MSH Steelhead Spawning Escapement Requirements," has not only resisted wild release regulations for West End rivers, he wanted to increase the number of wild fish anglers can kill on these rivers from five to 30 in 2000. The Olympic Peninsula's 24th district representative to the Washington legislature, Jim Buck—who previously played a major role in the firing of former WDFW director, Bern Shanks and opposed Elwha Dam removal—threatened to wrest control of the agency from the Fish and Wildlife Commission and return it to the legislature after some members showed an interest in wild release. The *Peninsula Daily News*, the peninsula's only daily newspaper, routinely publishes photographs of dead wild steelhead, and its outdoor columnist, Derrick Menekin, a Californian who moved to the peninsula several years ago, fawns over the anglers who kill large wild fish.

Of course, the advocates of wild kill have a right to argue that the WDFW knows what it is doing and that killing wild steelhead on the Olympic Peninsula is a good idea. They have made their sentiments known to the Commission in recent years:

"Frankly I never thought I would ever again see common sense and reliance on scientific data drive good decision making regarding this resource. I totally support the overall philosophy of permitting an increased opportunity to harvest wild steelhead stocks…"

"The department has offered liberalized regulations for harvest of wild steelhead based on scientific management for the Hoh, Quillayute and Queets/Clearwater river systems."

"With the sound scientific data now available, the department can manage these rivers to provide adequate spawning escapement and increased recreational harvest opportunity."

"They aren't bad people," said Bob Pigott. "They all caught wild fish and they all killed them. They want it to be the way it always was. But we used to have a lot more fish and a lot fewer fishermen. Now we have a lot fewer fish and a lot more fishermen. We just cannot keep killing wild fish."

Unfortunately, the words used by the defenders of wild harvest—science, escapement, sustainable harvest—have become so degraded by the WDFW over the years, so twisted to accommodate the demands of economic interests and political pressure from people like Jim Buck, as to be bereft of any practical meaning. This has become especially apparent in the years since the 1999 ouster of Bern Shanks, the first WDFW director in decades to place the health of the fish above the interests of anglers. Since then, long-time observers of Olympic Peninsula fish, fishing guides with decades of experience on these rivers, and many of the habitat biologists who know the rivers intimately have become openly skeptical, if not contemptuous, of virtually every pronouncement made by the WDFW.

Nowhere has the dissonance between the claims of the WDFW and the reality experienced by long-time West End anglers become more palpable than the controversy over Maximum Sustained Harvest. Maximum Sustained Harvest, which is also, confusingly, referred to as Maximum Sustained Yield, is the theory the agency uses to support its claim that there are thousands of "excess" wild steelhead available for harvest on Olympic Peninsula rivers.

"MSY seeks to take (harvest) a constant maximum surplus from the stock annually available for harvest, and to allow to escape to spawn the minimum number which is believed necessary to produce that maximum harvestable surplus," Washington Trout fisheries biologist, Nick Gayeski, wrote in a report the organization submitted to the Commission in advance of the vote on increasing wild harvest on West End rivers. "If all environmental and life-history conditions pertaining to the stock are constant (average), the successful implementation of MSY will result in a perpetual motion machine in which the annual spawning escapement is always the minimum necessary to produce the maximum harvestable surplus, and that surplus will always be harvested consistently and on an annual basis."

"The philosophy of Maximum Sustained Harvest has been killing us from the get go," Dick Goin told me, as we drank coffee in his home near the Olympic National Park visitor center in Port Angeles. "When you start a discussion on a false premise, everything that follows is false. The idea that these rivers are healthy and have adequate escapements is false. They officially adopted MSH in 1984, but have been managing that way since at least 1960. It deals with run estimates and it deals with redd counts. I was looking at redds when I was ten. I've done redd counting for the park. I've done it for the department. And I'll tell you one thing, it is always done with an axe to grind."

By way of example, Dick cites a friend who owns property on the East Twin River, one of the small, short-run winter steelhead systems that drains into the western Strait of Juan de Fuca. "He wanted to help, so he started counting redds," Dick said. According to Dick, the department advised his friend on what to count as redds. "It was ludicrous, the things they told him to count. There were false redds or "try" redds and places where maybe just an animal was crossing the creek." Dick's friend eventually did triumph, proving that the winter steelhead stock on the creek was much weaker than the WDFW claimed. "He got the East Twin closed," he said. "But they retaliated by proposing to open Deep Creek."

If redd counts are open to different interpretations and can be manipulated to satisfy an agenda, then the escapement goals set by the WDFW are even more controversial. Since the early 1980s, the agency's escapement targets—that is, the number of steelhead that it wants to survive to spawn—have been 5,900 on the Quillayute System rivers, 2,400 on the Hoh and 1,200 on the Quinault. An indication of the scientific precision of escapement methodology can best be seen on the Queets, where the state argues that the river needs 4,200 fish to be fully seeded, while the Quinault Tribe claims it is only 2,500. Moreover, the state and tribes have never settled on escapement targets for many creeks that flow into the Strait of Juan de Fuca, and the tribes do not accept the methods the state uses to determine esacapment. "I personally think they are way too low," Lower Elwha S'Klallam biologist Mike McHenry said.

"It's the same old story," Bob Pigott told me, when the

WDFW wanted to increase wild harvest in 2000. "We tell them there used to be more fish in the rivers and the biologists say 'How many?' and 'Can you prove it?' It's positively ridiculous. Any one of the Quillayute Rivers could support 5,900 steelhead alone."

A 2001 report by Peter Bahls for the Native Fish Society, "How Healthy Are Healthy Stocks?" suggests one way in which the escapement figures for the Sol Duc and other Quillayute rivers may be skewed on the low side. "The method assumes that the parr densities actually surveyed to derive the escapement estimate for a river were the result of an escapement yielding maximum recruitment," Bahls wrote. "It seems highly unlikely that parr densities during the surveys of the Sol Duc River in the late 1970s were at 'carrying capacity,' especially considering the significantly larger escapements in recent years." Indeed, the lowest wild Sol Duc escapement on record was in 1979, after the heavy incidental harvest of wild fish as a result of pressure directed at Chambers Creek hatchery steelhead.

Recently, the very premise behind MSH—that the number of steelhead a river is capable of producing over time is controlled largely by the amount of space that juvenile fish have for rearing—has also been seriously challenged. "Perhaps the greatest source of error in spawner-recruit model estimates is caused by the assumption that density-dependent factors are primarily responsible for determining survival (i.e., numbers of recruits per spawner)," Cederholm et al wrote in the 2001 report "Pacific Salmon and Wildlife": "There is ample evidence that environmental factors have a substantial effect on survival of salmon. In the freshwater environment survival may be affected by floods, droughts or declining habitat quality caused by numerous anthropogenic influences. There is growing evidence that productivity of the northern Pacific Ocean varies cyclically, greatly influencing mortality rates in the marine environment."

That MSH is an inherently risky way to manage steelhead, even when spawner numbers and escapement targets are precise, can be seen in the spawner/recruit curves the fish managers use to determine harvest targets. Basically, a spawner-recruit curve is a graphic representation of how many returning fish (recruits) will be produced by a specific number of spawners. The ascending 45-degree line across the graph represents the "replacement" of one recruit for each spawner, while the curve above the replacement represents the various points of other spawner/recruit scenarios. Obviously, the more adult fish you let spawn the more fish they produce. But, as we have seen, steelhead are considered "density dependent," and there is a point where each additional spawner results in progressively fewer juveniles. Managers determine the number of steelhead available for harvest under MSH by subtracting the number of spawners from the number of recruits.

Nick Gayeski created a hypothetical spawner/recruit curve for Hoh River winter steelhead in his 2000 presentation to the Commission. It showed that the Hoh produced a maximum of 4,800 steelhead when 3,200 fish were allowed to spawn. Under MSY, however, it only took 1,814 spawners to produce 4,203 fish. The number of fish available for harvest under MSY then was 2,389 steelhead. That is considerably more than the 1,600 (4,800-3,200) fish under the first strategy, but the danger occurs when the return is lower than predicted. If the run size was off by 20 percent, for example, producing only 3362 steelhead, and harvest was allowed at the MSY rate of 2,389, only 974 fish would be left to spawn. Those steelhead would, in turn, only produce 2,900 recruits—more than 1,300 fish below MSY targets. On the other hand, if 20 percent fewer fish (3,840) returned under the more conservative harvest strategy described above and 1,600 steelhead were still harvested, there would be 2,240 spawners instead of 3,200. These fish would produce 4,500, only 300 below the target of 4,800.

"Management of escapement and harvest based upon MSY must adequately account for this variability," Gayeski concluded. "So, of course, must any alternative approach. However, management at or near MSY is inherently more risky to the stock than less harvest-intensive management approaches. It places a high premium on the ability to estimate the total run size of the stock prior to the fishing season, leaving little margin for error in this estimate. In this sense, MSY management can be said to be knife-edge stock management."

More fundamentally, biologists have raised profoundly disturbing questions about the long-term implications of MSH. They point out that the loss of individual components of a stock, such as the West End's early-timed steelhead and tributary spawners, may diminish its adaptability in the face of changing environmental conditions. "Harvest policies and practices that inadvertently reduce or eliminate small population segments would decrease genetic variability and could impact stock productivity," Cederholm, et al. wrote in "Pacific Salmon and Wildlife." Managing for intentionally low numbers of spawners also limits the number of nutrient-rich salmon and steelhead carcasses in a river. "Therefore, if harvest of fish causes a reduction in nutrient delivery to the stream sufficient to impact growth, survival will be negatively impacted," Cederholm, et al. continued. "This impact will decrease recruitment to the next generation of spawners, further depleting the nutrient capital of the system and potentially further depressing survival."

Even more insidiously, the Washington Conservation Commission characterizes a system as possessing "healthy" biological processes if its escapement goals—goals that are widely disputed on Olympic Peninsula rivers—are regularly obtained.

Ultimately, MSH is similar to Chambers Creek hatchery steelhead in that it is a mechanism of biological impoverishment, a device created by managers that, in essence, shrinks the size of a river.

"I don't think it's working," said Olympic National Park biologist John Meyer. "The watersheds are too different. The ocean conditions have a huge effect on things, and there are hatchery fish all over the place. Hatchery fish can change the spawner/recruit curves. MSH pushes the fish population down to the edge. We certainly don't think it's successful."

Chapter Eighteen

Quinault

James Christie was probably the first person to lose a fly on a West End steelhead river. He lost it on the North Fork of the Quinault River in March of 1890, a few miles upstream of the confluence of the north and south forks. There would have been a lot of winter steelhead in the river at that time—bright late-returning fish, spawners with big kypes and crimson flanks, and thin dark kelts. But Christie wasn't fishing. After spending nearly six months on their historic first traverse of the Olympic Mountains by Euro-Americans, Christie and the other members of the Press Expedition had nothing more on their minds than to get out of the wilderness. Christie lost his flies when the driftwood raft they had cobbled together overturned, dumping not only his fly box but nearly the entire photographic record of the trip into the river. Given the nature of late 19th century fishing tackle, Christie's encounter with a North Fork winter steelhead would most likely have been over pretty quickly and pretty decisively, anyway.

The southernmost of the rainforest rivers, the Quinault River is as close to a perfect anadromous fish system as you are going to find. Flowing into the Pacific Ocean at Taholah, where the rocky points and bluffs of the north coast give way to the sandy beaches and bays of southwest Washington, it has one of the Olympic coast's largest estuaries. In its lower reaches, which lie within the Quinault Indian Nation, it is a series of corkscrew meanders and side channels. It is the only major West End river with a large lake on its mainstem. Above the lake, the cascades of its north fork and the gravel bars of the east fork maintain good flows throughout the year. The headwaters of the East Fork of the Quinault extend much further east than any other coastal river, all the way to Mount Anderson. Glacial water and snowmelt from Mount Anderson run west to the Pacific Ocean in the Quinault, north via the Elwha to the Strait of Juan de Fuca and east into the Dosewallips and, ultimately, Hood Canal.

"It can get too clear above the lake when it's cold and hasn't rained for a while," said Jay Brevik, a veteran of more than 20 years on the upper Quinault. "It is also pretty much a boat show. You can find a little bit of access at the bridge, but there is a lot of private property and it's a long distance between good water. You have to be careful in a boat, too. The river changes course after storms and there are a lot of dead-end channels and braids. It is important to get out and take a look if you don't know what's happening downstream. Also, you have to row across about a mile of the lake to reach the take-out and it can get nasty in the afternoon when the wind kicks up. It's a lot of work, but there are fish up there that are worth it."

Indeed, the Quinault Tribe netted a 37-pound winter steelhead during the 1980s, but every other migratory salmonid native to the West Coast south of Alaska also spawns in the Quinault River. It hosts strong populations of coho and spring/summer and fall chinook. Its estuary helps sustain the rain forest's largest chum and pink runs. Dolly Varden/bull trout range from tidewater to glacial rivulets, and densely-spotted cutthroat trout flourish as lake-dwellers, anadromous fish and resident trout. The systom's richest bounty, however, the fish that historically made the Quinault Indians the envy of tribes throughout the region, are its "blueback," or, as they are known today, sockeye salmon. The sockeye were so prized that settlers on the lower Columbia eventually erroneously applied the name "Quinaut" to all salmon, even chinook. The term is still in use in countries like New Zealand.

"The entrance of the Queniult is so badly blocked up with stones and gravel, piled up by the waves," James Swan wrote in his 1857 volume, *The Northwest Coast*, "that it is difficult of entrance except for canoes, and only for these during calm intervals; but once in the river, and it is found to be a beautiful little stream. The stopping of its mouth has caused the formation of a pretty little bay, where the water is as pure as crystal. Early in the spring, a species of small salmon enter this river, which are justly celebrated among all the Indians for their superior richness of flavor. This variety is from fourteen to twenty inches in length, rarely exceeding two feet, and weighs from five to ten pounds."

The clarity of the water that Swan remarked upon was partly a feature of the old-growth forest that dominated the Quinault basin at the time, which included the most magnificent stands of red cedar in the world. The upper Quinault River continues to run clearer today than its sister glacial rivers, and, as is nearly always the case on the Olympic Peninsula, that is a function of geography and geology. For while the lower river and lake lie within the rain forest, the Quinault headwaters drain the high country leeward of the Bailey Range and Skyline Ridge, the north/south windward spine of the Olympic Mountains. As a result, it receives less rainfall and snow. The Quinault basin drains 434 square miles, only slightly less than the Queets, and it actually has more stream miles and tributary length. Yet its record peak flow is 80,000 cubic feet per second, while the Queets' is 135,000 cfs.

Of all the West End rivers, the Quinault is probably the one where you are least likely to see a fly rod. Tribal guides are required on the reservation, and although some of the guides are accomplished fly-fishers, most of their business is with bait and gear anglers. Thousands of steelhead, both hatchery and wild, return to the lower river each winter, however, and it is an excellent place for a novice steelheader to connect with their first fish. Fewer fish swim upstream of the lake, but there are enough to make it more than worth the effort, and you do not need a guide in the upper river. While bank access is limited, it can be located, and you are not likely to have much competition.

"I fished it a few times last winter after they closed the Queets," Dave Steinbaugh said. "There is some beautiful water up there. There was no one around. I just hiked around. I had a great time."

Chapter Nineteen

Garrett's Stoneflies and Feather Wings

I have managed to live in some wonderful places on the Olympic Peninsula—a two-room cabin a stone's throw from the Elwha River; a trailer in the woods south of Port Townsend, the caretaker's cabin at the Dungeness National Wildlife Refuge. Currently, my wife, Ellie, and I and our yellow Labrador, Lily, and grouchy cat, Max, live a couple of hundred yards from Dabob Bay. Roosevelt elk appear at regular intervals; we have watched young calves nursing in summer and heard the reedy whistle of bulls and the clack of antlers during the fall rut. We can hear sea lions in spring, brant during the winter, and eagles most of the year. It's easily the best place I have stumbled onto in my adult life.

But in terms of fly-fishing for steelhead, the pitched-roof home where Olympic Peninsula fly-tying master, Jim Garrett, lived on the Sol Duc has any place I have ever lived beaten. Located on the infamous "Bear Creek" drift on the upper river, it was the staff housing for the hatchery technician that maintained the Washington Department of Fisheries' (WDF) old Bear Springs salmon hatchery. This section of river tends to be avoided by all but the most accomplished oarsmen, especially during low water, and it is above the deadline for salmon fishing, which reduces crowding, but the steelhead have no problem reaching it boulder-strewn riffles and tailouts. The house is the kind of place where you can walk out into the front yard, take a quick glance at the water level, and decide if you want to make a few casts before supper.

The creator of dozens of flies designed specifically for Olympic Peninsula steelhead, trout and salmon, Jim Garret emerged as the region's fly-tying exemplar after Syd Glasso retired to Seattle in the late 1970s. Unlike Glasso, who worked alone or with a small group of friends, Garrett's era of influence coincided with the phenomenal expansion of fly-fishing that began in the late 1970s and

1980s. He helped nurture a generation of fly-fishers with his popular fly-tying classes at Peninsula College and Manuel Bernardo's Quality Fly Fishing Shop in Port Angeles. When the first Olympic Peninsula chapter of the Federation of Fly Fishers was organized in the early 1980s, it elected him president. Garrett and the club were instrumental in securing the upper Hoko River as "fly-only" water, the first fly water for winter steelhead in the state of Washington. "Jim had a sort of love affair with the Hoko," J.D. Love recalled.

A meticulous craftsman who approached Glasso's stature as an artisan, Garrett was the Olympic Peninsula's first great fly-tying naturalist. Some of Garrett's most brilliant patterns are intimately-conceived representations of the insects that inhabit Olympic Peninsula rivers. Garrett's close observations of subaquatic insects came about in part as an outgrowth of his having lived not only on the banks of the Sol Duc, but also on the Dungeness and Elwha rivers during his career with the WDF. This gave him contact with the most important insects for Olympic steelhead and trout, specifically the salmonfly, golden stones and October caddis. In this way, he forged a connection between Olympic Peninsula fly patterns and the small tradition of representative steelhead flies such as the Steelhead Bee and the Pewan Nymph.

Because the overwhelming bulk of insect activity on the peninsula occurs between mid-spring and late autumn, as it does everywhere else, many of Garrett's flies are designed with summer steelhead and cutthroat in mind. The color plates in Trey Combs' *Steelhead Fly Fishing and Flies* reveal the elegance and simple beauty of Garrett's soft-hackle flies in his Montana series, his low-water patterns like the Peterson, egg patterns such as the Trinity, and his dressings designed to imitate the larval and adult forms of the October caddis. These are lovely flies, evocative of the early dressings on the Rogue, Umpqua and Klamath, and they are excellent during the low water of mid to late summer.

Other than a sprinkling of *Baetis* mayflies and small dark stoneflies, there is minimal insect activity either above or below the surface on the Olympic Peninsula during the winter. But the West End's maritime climate is considerably less severe than most comparable northern latitudes, and the lower and mid-elevation reaches of the rivers typically warm up enough by March and early

April to stimulate insect activity, even hatches. Salmonflies often appear over the larger West End streams, especially the Quillayute System rivers, by mid April, weeks before they emerge on the Deschutes or Yellowstone area rivers. Although the golden stoneflies won't hatch until summer, the nymphs presumably begin moving around on the bottom during spring, as well.

For winter steelheaders, this quickening pace of insect activity was more remarked about than acted upon until Jim Garrett created his Orange and Black Olympic Stonefly Nymph in the early 1970s. This is understandable, because you can spend an awful lot of time wading Quillayute and rainforest rivers without ever seeing an adult steelhead take a swipe at a salmonfly. But stoneflies are an important part of the drift that steelhead grow up with as juveniles, and they most likely comprise a significant portion of the steelhead's pre-smolt diet. On California rivers, nymphs such as Brindle Bugs, the Pewan Nymph and the ubiquitous Woolly Bugger have accounted for thousands of fish since the 1960s. It seemed reasonable that adult steelhead that routinely hit shrimp and salmon eggs, not to mention corkies and Hot Shots and Little Cleos, would be just as likely to snatch up a stonefly nymph.

Syd Glasso, himself, presaged the use of flies that are suggestive of insects in springtime. In his fly selection recommendations in Trey Combs' *Steelhead Fly Fishing and Flies*, Glasso distinguished between patterns for winter and those for March and April on Quillayute System rivers. The Orange Heron and Sol Duc Dark that he recommended for spring are considerably more naturalistic and "buggy" than the brighter and more fluorescent dressings in the Sol Duc series. It doesn't take much imagination to picture these flies—or the even more somber Brown Heron, Gold Heron and Black Heron—as drowned stoneflies, drifting legs akimbo in the current. Further it is interesting that Glasso didn't make seasonal distinctions for the Hoh and Queets, glacial systems that are typically less clear than the Quillayute rivers and where increased flooding and scour may reduce insect productivity.

The task Jim Garrett set for himself when he created his Orange and Black Olympic Stonefly was qualitatively different from tiers who developed impressionistic representations of insects: He wanted an imitation that actually looked like a stonefly nymph. No, his goal was even more rigorous than that: He wanted a fly that looked like a *Pteronarcys californica*. Unlike the more well-known stonefly nymphs available at the time, which limited themselves to suggesting a stonefly with broad brush strokes, Garrett's nymph had antennae and feelers and eyes and distinct body segments and an orange thorax. It was the most impressive stonefly nymph any steelheader had ever seen. It looked like it had just crawled up onto a streamside rock on a sunny April afternoon. If Garret had been a painter, he would have been one of those Dutch artists who painted the eerily realistic clocks and dogs and burghers.

In the three decades since Garrett first introduced his Olympic stoneflies, nymphs have become a standard part of the springtime repertoire of Quillayute System anglers. Most fly-fishers present them as Garrett did, casting upstream, throwing a large mend, then fishing them dead-drift until they come under the influence of the current. A few veterans of his classes still tie the Olympic Black and Orange Stonefly, including the series of color variations that he told Trey Combs were inspired by the Hot Shot plugs so effective on Olympic rivers. As with Glasso's Spey flies, the demanding nature of Garrett's stoneflies and their rather specialized materials have limited the number of anglers who tie them. Today, most steelhead fly-fishers have absorbed the larger lessons of Garrett's nymphs, but many young and visiting anglers who routinely fish Bitch Creeks and Montana Stones on these rivers have never heard of the Black and Orange Stonefly.

Although they are even less well known than his stoneflies, Garrett's feather-winged dressings are my favorites. Originally created for summer steelhead and low-water winter fish, these flies trace their lineage directly to the very earliest steelhead dressings. Indeed, other than the heightened colors available through hot dyes and fluorescents, the materials that Garrett utilized would have been familiar to John Benns in the early 1900s or Vancouver Island's General Money in the 1920s. Garrett's Kate, for example, has the same green-winged teal flank, jungle cock cheeks and palmered hackle as Benns' Railbird. Similar to General Money's spare and elegant dressings for Vancouver Island's Stamp River, Garrett's feather wings also employed golden pheasant and goose quill. On the hook, the appeal of these materials is subtle, a far cry from the screaming assertiveness of many contemporary winter steelhead flies. It is this quality that makes them ideal for low-water springtime steelheading.

Feather wings, of course, are not very durable, even less so than Spey flies, and that is the main reason they fell out of favor after bucktail came into prominence as a material. But West End rivers are not only usually warmer during March and April, they are also often lower and clearer. The frequency and intensity of rainfall usually falls off steeply after mid-February, but temperatures in the high country remain cold enough to hold off the snowmelt until May or June. Steelhead holding lies are often more shallow than they have been since October, or will be again until mid-summer. This is when shorter, lighter sink-tips perform well over broad tailouts and slots, and many times floating lines are the most effective line of all. It is the perfect time to fish a Garrett feather wing.

The period when Garrett's stoneflies and feather wings are most effective on West End rivers, of course, coincides with the time when many wild steelhead take up positions on spawning beds. There is an incredible mixture of steelhead on the rivers during March and April—bright late-arriving wild fish, early summer steelhead, and colored-up fish that have been in the river for a while but that still won't spawn for weeks. But there are a lot of spawners, and it is critical that fly-fishers avoid disturbing them. It is not ethical, obviously, but it is also just plain stupid, because it gives the enemies of fly-fishing, and especially wild-steelhead release, ammunition in their strange and vengeful quest to have the late-season and headwaters areas of these rivers closed. It is easy to avoid spawners. Steelhead prefer relatively shallow water for spawning, and they seek out gravel bottoms. It is a good idea to avoid these areas entirely and, instead, concentrate on pockets, slots and shelves, and the holding areas above and below rapids where traveling fish rest.

I can't think of any better way to spend a spring day than on the Sol Duc, Bogachiel or Calawah with a box of Garrett feather wings. After more than four months of struggling with heavy sink-tips, huge flies and swollen rivers, the opportunity to fish floating lines and elegant flies is as liberating as throwing off a heavy back-pack after climbing up to a mountain lake. The low water you encounter this time of year also often keeps drift boats off all but the lowest reaches of the rivers, setting you up for a day of solitude and fresh fish. Even better, flies like the Kate and D'Ana Marie have an understated, luminous quality that seems perfectly attuned to springtime—to the soft vaguely green water and the slanting shafts of sunshine filtered through Sitka spruce boughs.

The fact that these graceful dressings are the creation of a dedicated Olympic Peninsula angler who loved these rivers dearly is nothing but frosting on the cake.

Chapter Twenty

Timber and Fish

It rained a lot on the West End during December of 1999. Upwards of five inches fell on the Hoh River basin on December 15 alone. Falling in dense, nearly opaque curtains, it triggered a series of landslides on slopes and ridges that were already saturated. Unstable slopes below high-elevation logging roads sloughed off waves of mud and trees and rock, collapsing ultimately into the Hoh mainstem or South Fork of the Hoh. Defective culverts backed up the swollen flow of headwater tributaries until they blew out, sending torrents of water toward the Hoh. There were "ridge to river" failures on Winfield Creek and Owl Creek, and a collapsed culvert on Dismal Creek destroyed 90 percent of the basin. All in all, over 30 landslides were documented in the Hoh Valley alone.

"Every main tributary on this ridge has failed numerous times," said Jill Silver, pointing to the Washington Department of Natural Resources (DNR) land on Heulsdonk Ridge south of the Hoh River. "There were debris flows on all of these tributaries in December."

A habitat biologist with the Hoh Indian Tribe, Jill has spent years inventorying, monitoring and defending fish habitat in the Hoh basin. She had agreed to lead a tour of the "managed," that is, logged, portion of the middle Hoh to discuss the new Forests and Fish Report. It is the new set of forestry guidelines passed by the Washington legislature and that the National Marine Fisheries Service had agreed were adequate to protect ESA-listed species. We were joined by our friends, Jerry Gorsline and his wife Beth McBarron. Jerry is a policy analyst with the Washington Environmental Council, and Beth is a long-time salmon activist. The state's premier salmonid advocacy organization, Washington Trout, was represented by its executive director, Kurt Beardslee, and my friend and its public information officer, Ramon Vanden Brulle.

"It's usually sunny on the Hoh when it's raining to the north," Jill said, as we bounced down the Owl Creek Road.

Red salmonberry blossoms and Indian plum tassels had climbed up out of the river bottoms onto the terraces and ridges by the time we made it to the Hoh, but there was nothing vernal and certainly no sense of renewal about the scene we beheld when we pulled off next to Iron Maiden Creek. A small mainstem tributary that flows into the Hoh between Owl Creek and the South Fork of the Hoh, its flow that day would barely cover the instep on a pair of hiking boots, but it had raged down Huelsdonk Ridge with the energy of an out-of-control locomotive in December. Its stream bed was a gouged chute of bedrock, bare dirt and boulders, some the size of small cars. There were no standing trees or even shrubs next to the river; full-grown trees, some four or five feet in diameter, criss-crossed the channel in chaotic jackstraw piles. Enormous root wads dangled a dozen feet above the ground.

"One of the things I told Forests and Fish was that you have to deal with the west side of the Olympics differently than the rest of western Washington because of the rain," Jill said, as we piled back into the Jeep. "But that didn't happen."

We spent the day exploring both sides of the middle Hoh. Jill led us down a soggy skid road to an engineered log jam near the mouth of the South Fork. Ramon observed that the logs within the jam were larger than any they saw on the east side of Puget Sound. We drove to the bottom end of Iron Maiden Creek, where it had nearly taken out a trailer on its free-fall to the valley floor and where the riparian zone was now indistinguishable from a gravel pit. Kurt pointed out the shriek of a pileated woodpecker, and Beth identified water parsley for me. Later, we poked around a forested wetland on the north side of the river. The ground was so sodden and so broken up with elk tracks that we had to run to keep from sinking into the muck. Through it all, I was haunted by Jill's remark that things happen differently on the West End, and that Forests and Fish had ignored that single fact.

"We found a hemlock stump that is less than eight inches wide but that is more than 300 years old," Jill said. "It was in a forested wetland." It obviously hadn't grown very tall in that time, yet with the forest practices regulations proposed under Forests and Fish it would have been subject to harvest at 100 years of age, or less.

Logging is the dominant industry on the West End of the Olympic Peninsula, and bushellers and choke setters, hook tenders and yarders perform honorable, complicated and dangerous work. However "historic logging practices," as the forestry-school graduates and MBAs genteely refer to them, made virtually no provisions for fish habitat. Early logging reached a dubious climax of sorts in the 1920s, when the Bureau of Indian Affairs authorized non-tribal interests to harvest tens of thousands of acres on the Quinault Indian Nation without either replanting the trees or removing the enormous slash piles. In addition to obliterating the finest old-growth red cedar groves in the world, these operations resulted in huge fires that devastated large areas of the reservation for decades. Logging practices gradually improved after that, but as the easily accessible river bottom forests played out in the 1940s, the industry began to use trucks and logging roads to push higher and higher into the foothills. By the 1960s, the last large tract of old-growth timber on the Olympic Peninsula was on the steep DNR land between the Queets and Hoh rivers. Upwards of 2 billion board feet of lumber rolled off those hillsides on a network of log roads by 1971.

The high-elevation slopes were more unstable than the lower-elevation forests, and in the spring of 1971 two slides below new logging roads devastated Stequaleho Creek, a major Clearwater River tributary. The DNR responded with a series of studies on the effects of timber harvest on salmon habitat, and it began paving main haul roads and eliminating the practice of "side casting" soil excavated during road building onto the slopes. The damage was already done. When 18 inches of rain fell on the upper Hoh within a 24-hour period in November of 1990, it triggered a massive series of slope failures along Huelsdonk Ridge. An estimed 243,000 cubic yards of sediment came off the ridge during the storm, and more than one-third of it made it all the way down to the South Fork of the Hoh. This time a Slope Stability Task Force was organized, and it accumulated evidence on the effects of logging on steep slopes:

Mass wasting due to roads results in 168 times the erosion as landslides in undisturbed areas.

The percent of sediment in the water is correlated to the presence of roads. Fine sediment levels in spawning gravels in tributaries and side channels of the South Fork of the Hoh were, respectively, 41 and 20 percent, while comparable areas in Olympic National Park were 9 and 12 percent.

The abundance and diversity of macro invertebrates in the South Fork Hoh were between 40 and 75 percent less than in similar habitat in park rivers.

In the decades since the first Clearwater slide, Washington politicians have grudgingly imposed a series of regulatory mechanisms on the timber industry. The first was the 1974 Forest Practices Act. Although habitat degradation continued, eventually resulting in the listing of the Northern spotted owl, an old-growth-dependent species, as an endangered species, it allowed public comment and litigation on contested timber sales. Then in the 1980s, after Indian tribes successfully argued that the state had a legal obligation to protect the habitat that supported fish, the tribes helped organize the Timber-Fish-Wildlife Agreement, an ostensibly more collaborative approach. The most recent effort, the 1999 Forests and Fish Report, emerged when it became clear that a whole host of Washington salmon and steelhead populations would join the spotted owl on the list of endangered species.

Unfortunately, by the time we toured the middle Hoh with Jill, it had become clear that Forests and Fish had much more to do with preserving the uninterrupted flow of timber-industry profits than with protecting steelhead and salmon habitat. Indeed, several Indian tribes, including the Hoh, and the entire environmental delegation had withdrawn from the negotiations in protest before they were completed. They argued that, if anything, Forests and Fish was a retrenchment from Timber-Fish-Wildlife. Among other things, it locked the terms of the agreement in place for 50 years, regardless of any changes in environmental conditions or status of the fish. It also eliminated any river-specific measures, such as the Watershed Analysis for the Middle Hoh that was 90 percent complete before Forests and Fish. It also exempted small timber owners from some of its requirements, and its protection of riparian zones and steep slopes were minimal at best.

"There are over 100 blocking culverts in the Hoh Basin," Jill said. "Under Forests and Fish, the DNR has 15 years to fix them." This is despite the fact that they are already clearly illegal. "Now the timber companies are applying for public funds to repair them. And the orphaned roads, the abandoned roads built before the

Forest Practices Act, all they have to do is inventory and assess them. On the Goodman Creek basin, there are one to four miles of road for every square mile outside of Olympic National Park. Seventy percent of them block fish passage."

"The point of the regulatory system is that it is supposed to work," Jerry said. "There is supposed to be mitigation."

Of all people, Washington anglers probably have the best perspective on the machinations behind Forests and Fish because they have had experience with three of the report's most important negotiators. Bruce Wilkerson, the representative of the aggressive pro-logging lobby, the Washington Forest Protection Association, was previously the director of the Washington Department of Fisheries. Representing Governor Gary Locke, Washington's "salmon czar," Curt Smitch, was a former director of the Washington Department of Fish and Wildlife, and worked for Wilkerson at one time. Bob Turner, the northwest director of the National Marine Fisheries Service, the agency that signed off on Forests and Fish as adequate for ESA habitat protection, was also, incredibly, a colleague of Wilkerson's at the WDF.

As Olympic Peninsula author and naturalist, Tim McNulty, wrote in *Forest* Magazine, "These, in fact, were the same managers who presided over the salmon's decline."

For his part, Wilkerson is proud of their work. "Every negotiator was supported by a science team," he told McNulty, "and every scientist in the room was in agreement. When they said, 'This will work,' we stopped negotiating."

That isn't how the scientists at the American Fisheries Society saw it, though:

"A document intended to be based on sound science would provide documentation from the scientific literature to support each of the document's conclusions. Not only does the Report contain no supporting citations, but also it does not describe rationales used to develop the recommended prescriptions. Science-based information is presented only in the definitions accompanying the Report, and a surprising portion of the information presented is inaccurate.

"Because the Report cites no scientific literature, the credibility of the Report rests solely on the credibility and expertise of the Report's authors. That the authors appear to be ill-informed concerning disciplines on which the Report is founded undermines the credibility of the Report itself."

The consequences of Forests and Fish will reverberate through Washington forests for decades, but its impact will be especially profound for the Hoh Tribe and Hoh River steelhead and salmon. With its reservation only encompassing a square mile at the mouth of the river, the tribe has neither a significant timber income, like the Quinault to the south, nor a growing tourism economy, as do the Quileute to the north. The fate of the Hoh Tribe is tethered intimately to the river's runs of salmon and steelhead, and the fish depend upon the healthy functioning of the watershed. The tribe's share of the spring/summer chinook run in 1999 was only 62 fish. In the Hoh, as is the case on the other rainforest rivers, the productivity of the watershed is inextricably linked to its abundance of large trees and wetlands. Yet of the more than 500 miles of tributaries within the basin that do not currently contain fish, only approximately one-half will receive any protection under proposed Forests and Fish rules.

In its April, 2000 response to the Draft Environmental Impact Statement for Forest Practices Rules under Forests and Fish, the Hoh Tribe concluded that the preferred alternative relied on "experimental strategies and scientifically unsupported theories, and omits many important components necessary to protect species and their habitat." It specifically cited concerns over: 1) the issue of windthrow in riparian zones; 2) the lack of monitoring of sediment delivery from roads; 3) the absence of prescriptions regarding mass-wasting and unstable slopes and 4) the adoption of riparian buffers that are not supported by any scientific evidence and that are incapable of being monitored or enforced.

"High risk to fish, fish habitat, water quality, water quantity, macroinvertebrate abundance and diversity is especially inherent in the lack of buffers on headwater streams and the limited treatment of 'sensitive sites'," the tribe concluded.

For those of us who spend our time wandering around the Hoh with fly rods, it is sometimes a little abstract to connect, say, sediment loads or riparian buffers with the number of steelhead or salmon in the river. Culverts are a simple and easily understandable way to see the relationship between habitat degrading activities and salmonid production. An impassable culvert on a spawning tributary, after all, functions in exactly the same way as a dam without fish passage. In a 1997 petition to Jefferson County, Jill quantified the impact of 10 blocking culverts on county roads. Repairing these culverts alone, according to Jill, could produce potentially 81 additional steelhead annually. When you realize that the escapement goal for the entire Hoh System is only 2,400 wild winter steelhead, that becomes significant. In addition to culverts, Jill has documented 37 cedar splats—debris left in the stream after cedar salvage that obstructs fish passage and degrades water quality—in the Hoh basin alone.

I ran into Jill a few times after our trip to the Hoh, but two springtimes came and went before we had a chance to sit down and talk about how Forests and Fish was working out on the ground. There was good news. "We had coho all over the place last year," she said, with a twinkle in her eyes. "And in streams not considered fish-bearing under Forests and Fish." But she said the timber companies and DNR were pushing the already-weak legislation as far as they could. In arguably the sleaziest attempt of all, some companies attempted to claim that tributaries that were without fish during the drought summer of 2001 should be downgraded permanently to "non-fish bearing" status. The Department of Natural Resources also tried to downgrade an 800-foot reach of a Hoh River tributary that had been identified as capable of restoration. Jill won that battle.

"We've been set back," she said. "We've lost some protection we had. The biggest thing about Forests and Fish is that it will maintain degraded conditions across the landscape. There are functions that are happening on the landscape that are poorly provided for in the rules."

Perhaps the ultimate legacy of Forests and Fish is that it will further diminish the productivity of the Hoh and other West End rivers. Each debris torrent that scours a tributary will not only eliminate fish from that stream for the short term; it may very well remove it from production permanently, because the meager habitat protections on small streams will prevent many from recovering. Every time a forested wetland is harvested it will jeopardize the groundwater transfers that sustain critical overwintering habitat for steelhead, coho and cutthroat trout. And as the oldest and largest trees are removed from the basin, it will steadily lose the snags and woody debris that function as its skeletal system. In this way, Forests and Fish functions in remarkable tandem with current WDFW harvest and hatchery policies. Like them, it will effectively shrink the river over time, creating a spiral of depletion, of less abundance, less genetic diversity and less biological complexity. Worst of all, it will impair the basin's capacity to restore and heal its wounds, something it has been doing for thousands of years.

Over the course of the long and acrimonious timber wars on the Olympic Peninsula during the 1980s, when the timber industry and environmental groups wrangled over the remaining old growth, a lot of wildly, and oftentimes intentionally, inaccurate claims were made on both sides of the debate. I remember a letter to a local newspaper decrying the "devastation" of the clear-cuts south of US 101 in the Sol Duc drainage and mourning the tragic loss of the "ancient" forest that would have stood there otherwise. In reality, these forests had already been dramatically affected by a hurricane force windstorm in 1921, which destroyed an estimated 3 billion cubic yards of timber, and the 1951 Forks Fire, which burned 18 miles, to the edge of town, in 12 hours. There are substantial areas of the middle Sol Duc mainstem and North Fork of the Calawah where I am older than the most "ancient" trees.

On the other hand, the old Forest Service/Park Service office near the Shuwah Pool displayed a poster that promoted the sophistry that harvest of old-growth forests was necessary to prevent the waste associated with "overmature" trees. That such a preposterously silly notion could be uttered with a straight face within a forty-minute drive of the Hoh rain forest, one of the most magnificent stands of "unmanaged" trees on the planet, certainly deserves some sort of award for self-interested wrongheadedness. As Robert Pyle wrote in *Wintergreen*, "Forests did manage to replace themselves, somehow prior to the advent of modern forestry."

Perhaps the most eloquent and most accurate statements uttered during that whole sorry controversy were the small signs with yellow letters in West End yards and windows that proclaimed, "This Family Supported by Timber Industry Dollars."

It has become increasingly clear in recent years, however, that the anadromous fish of the Olympic Peninsula, whether on the Hoh, Deep Creek, the Dickey or the North Fork of the Calawah, are, like the logging families, timber-dependent species themselves.

"My main goal now is to do research to identify areas, particularly headwaters and groundwater, that are gaps in the regulations," Jill said. "Forests and Fish ignores the processes that transfer from the top to the bottom of a watershed and they all produce fish."

Chapter Twenty-one

DixwodAchtada

Although you would never know it today, the Dickey River watershed once hummed with human activity. There was at least one permanent Quileute Indian village on the river before 1900, at the mouth of Coal Creek, and the tribe maintained four fish weirs on the mainstem Dickey. Trails lead from the East Dickey to the Quillayute Prairie, where the Indians dug camas and other roots, and up the West Fork to Dickey Lake, where they fished, hunted and gathered berries and grasses for baskets. A path from Gunderson Creek on the East Fork connected to Schuwah, allowing the tribal members to visit friends and relatives on the Sol Duc. They hunted elk on the East Fork between the confluence and Thunder Creek, poling upriver in canoes, then drifting down at sunrise or dusk. They also fished for the prized blueback, or sockeye, salmon in the lakes of the West Fork—Wentworth and Big Joe's lakes. In 1908, Quileute tribal member Sixtis Ward traded smelt and clams for butter and potatoes from Mina Smith, a Caucasian single mother who operated a 147-acre homestead just above the junction of the east and west forks. The name Dickey is a corruption of the Quileute word for the river—DixwodAchtada.

"We moved out there as elk country in 1959, after we left the Calawah," Dick Goin recalled. "We could usually find a log, an old-growth spruce to cross the river in the old days. It was never-never land from there to the ocean. The west, middle and east forks are all different. The East Fork had a lot of rock shelves and many deep holes. There was old-growth Sitka spruce in the log jams, huge trees. The West Fork has a falls. Did you know that? It's slower. It's quite pretty. Even then there weren't many steelhead. There was pressure from nets on the Quillayute River. All of the pressure from the nets affected the Dickey. But I saw it when it had a lot of coho. Dickey steelhead were spectacular fish. They were always short and thick. We hooked and lost some that went from large to huge. Some of the nastiest fish were on the Dickey."

There is no other West Coast anadromous fish system in the lower 48 states remotely like the Dickey River. A huge sprawling complex of freshwater sloughs, spongy wetlands and brushy creeks, it is fed by rainfall, springs, lakes and cedar swamps. In a region dominated by foothills and mountains, the Dickey watershed is amazingly flat, with scarcely a thousand-foot ridgeline in the basin. It is, in essence, a cold northern Everglades, transporting the rainfall of one of the wettest places on the planet in slow inexorable sheets to the Quillayute River. It historically supported strong runs of chinook, chum and sockeye salmon, along with sea-run cutthroat and winter steelhead. But its low gradient and mazes of off-channel rearing habitat were ideal for coho salmon, and even today, after some of the most aggressive logging in the Northwest, it is still one of the most productive coho systems in the state.

"I've seen good numbers of salmon on the very uppermost tributary sections," Buck Adamire told me several years ago. "Those coho swim to some areas to spawn where one would think it impossible." Indeed, he said that years ago at a logging show on Sands Creek, a tributary to Dickey Lake, a crew member discovered salmon in the creek. "A quick check upstream in the unlogged portion of the stream contained salmon too. End result was we moved the tower where (there was) no stream and again no timber was removed until June 1st."

Recent scientific investigations of Dickey River winter steelhead have identified a genetic marker that is found in no other Quillayute System steelhead, or any other Olympic Peninsula steelhead, for that matter. Unfortunately, the Lower Elwha S'Klallam's 1996 report, "Status of Salmon and Their Habitats on the Olympic Peninsula, Washington," described Dickey steelhead as "threatened." It listed five principle causes: logging, stream clearing, estuary impacts, mixed stock harvest and terminal harvest. Fish passage problems due to culverts and predation on juvenile steelhead (and coho) is also a problem. Wild harvest is still, unaccountably, legal on the Dickey, with February and March the most productive months in recent years. Although there are no current hatchery plants, roughly one-third of the fish taken in recent years have been hatchery fish, yet another indication of the straying tendencies of cultured fish.

"It's just pathetic what is happening out there," Dick said. "It's silting in incredibly . . . It's failing very rapidly now. Squawfish are a problem. I know they are in the West Fork and have caught them in the Middle Fork and have reliable information they are in the East Fork, too. I don't know why they are spreading, but it may be because the rivers are shallow and warm now. The lake is terrible. I don't know how any fry get through."

Despite the fact that there aren't very many steelhead and that much of the basin looks like the site of a nuclear accident, I continue to be tugged by the Dickey's subtle charm. Years ago, I liked to fish it by bicycle. I had a very sturdy, balloon-tired one-speed back then, and I would drag it across the East Fork and explore the network of log roads upstream. More recently, Ellie and I have developed a tradition of spending a couple of days at the Ocean Park Resort at La Push for my birthday in March. There are a wealth of steelheading options available from that base—the lower Sol Duc and Bogachiel, the Quillayute itself, Goodman Creek—but I nearly always spend a day on the Dickey.

Most of the time Ellie sleeps in and walks on the beach, but she occasionally accompanies me to the river. I remember one time in particular. It was unseasonably cold, and there was a heavy coat of frost on the steamside alders. Ellie was getting over a cold and said she would stay in the truck and read. I slipped my old down vest over my fly vest. I strung my 8-weight with a floating line and tied on a weighted Glo Bug. I scooted carefully down the icy bank to the river and began wading upstream. I hiked across sand bars and along the shallow edge of the river for about a half mile before I began to fish.

Because it is so close to the coast, the Dickey has a different feel than the other Quillayute System rivers. Truly large Sitka spruce are rare these days, and the intense winds from the ocean snap the tops off many of the remaining conifers. The big leaf maple are heavily festooned with moss and licorice fern, as in the rain forest, and the alder wear a white coat of lichen, giving them a ghostly appearance when fog drifts in from the beach, a scant three miles to the west. The water is clear but carries the iced-tea stain of its swampy origins. The entire basin, in fact, has the feel of a swamp, with water draining and percolating from seemingly every direction. In the spring, the buds on the alders give them a red appearance from a distance. In March, the brilliant yellow bracts of skunk cabbage appear, and you hear the year's first frogs.

"It's a really interesting river," said Jerry Gorsline, who represented the Washington Environmental Council in a watershed analysis of the river for Timber-Fish-Wildlife in the early 1990s. "It's so flat out there, the fish can get just about everywhere. We would find fish everywhere there was water. When we did surveys, we figured if there was water, there were fish."

I took my time fishing back downstream that day. It was cold in the river bottom, and I could see my breath. I hooked a small dark steelhead that wasn't much bigger than a large sea-run cutthroat, but lost it almost immediately on a snag. I was in a good mood when I got back to the road, though, and was ready to return to the cabin for corned beef hash and eggs, another birthday tradition.

Ellie wasn't in the truck, and my stomach lurched hollowly for a moment. Then, looking around quickly, I spotted her big green parka and her brown hair peaking out its top. Moving more closely, I saw the rise and fall of her coat that indicated she was breathing. She was lying up against a brushy bank and was sound asleep in a slanting patch of late-morning sun. I often tease her about being a heliotropic species. I realized that as the sun had tracked away from the truck, she had followed it across the road.

"Hey," I said, gently touching her shoulder.

"Oh, hi," she said, knuckling her eyes. "I must have fallen asleep."

"You want to go back?"

She nodded, then shivered. "Yeah. I'm cold."

We got in the truck, and I started it. She worked the levers of the heater. We rode in silence for a few minutes, as the heater worked on the cab. When I pulled up to the stop sign at the corner by the cemetery, she looked at me and smiled.

"Are you having a good day, birthday man?"

I nodded. "The best."

Chapter Twenty-two

Calawah

A seven-mile reach of the North Fork of the Calawah River runs dry each summer. It is a natural phenomenon, the result of porous rock and the gravel outwash nature of that section of the river. For the Quileute Indians, the tribe that controlled the vast Quillayute System watershed before whites came to the region, the drying reach was a sacred place. The Indians knew that the water didn't simply vanish, that it went underground, then reappeared downstream. They believed that the area possessed spiritual power and that it was a place of transformation for humans as well as the river. It became a destination for vision quests and was seen as the place where the souls of the departed passed on their way to the land of the dead.

"Early settlers found a partially-finished canoe along the bank there," John McMillan said. "Some people said that they just didn't finish it. But that's not the way Indians did things. They didn't build half a canoe then abandon it. The canoe was the vehicle for transporting the soul to the afterlife. The half of it that was finished was for this part of the journey, the part in this world, and the other half was for the part of the journey that we can't see."

The word Calawah, itself, is an Indian word that translates as "in the middle." Heading up between the Bogachiel and the Sol Duc basins, the Calawah watershed indeed drains the middle portion of the Quillayute System. Its extreme headwaters are encircled like a hanging valley by Rugged Ridge, Hunger Mountain and Biggler Mountain. Its North Fork flows more or less parallel to the mainstem Sol Duc, hidden behind Calawah Ridge, and the South Fork, which is largely within Olympic National Park, traces a vaguely westward course just across the ridge from the Bogachiel River. The South Fork's principle tributary, Sitkum River, runs between the north and south fork and actually drains a larger area than the north fork.

The forks meet on Olympic National Forest land a couple of miles south of the Smoke House Restaurant north of Forks. On the final leg of its journey, the mainstem Calawah meanders between the rapidly converging courses of the Sol Duc and Bogachiel, finally emptying into the Bogachiel a mile or so below the Bogachiel Rearing Pond and within a mile, as the crow flies, of the Sol Duc.

"The old-timers have told me that in the old days nobody in Forks even bothered to fish the Sol Duc or Bogachiel," Bob Pigott said. "The Calawah was on the outskirts of town and that was all the farther anybody felt they needed to go. It had all the fish they wanted."

During the winter, wild harvest is legal on the mainstem below Highway 101, and any type of tackle is permitted. Wild release and selective fishery regulations are in effect above the highway, although at times they seem honored more in the breach than in practice. Above the forks, the South Fork remains open through February up to Sitkum River, while the North Fork is closed in the winter.

For anglers from outside the Olympic Peninsula, the Calawah has always flowed not only literally but also figuratively in the shadow of its larger neighbors. But from Syd Glasso down to the new generation of fly-anglers like John McMillan, the Calawah has always been revered for both its large late wild winter steelhead, and for its unique character. A clearer, slower river than the other major West End systems, it occasionally carries the tea-colored stain of the creeks, even during winter at low flows. Gravel bars are smaller and less frequent than on the Bogachiel to the south, where the slightly heavier rainfall creates a more rambunctious river. But it is different from the Sol Duc, as well, with a slower flow and less gradient in most areas. It is a river of bedrock shelves and dark pools and long riffles.

"I'll tell you, I love the Calawah," said Jim Kerr, fly-fishing guide and proprietor of the Port Townsend Angler. "It has a lot of real nice fly water and the access is good. That's where I go when I want to fish in a traditional way, when I want to swing flies and fish traditional steelhead patterns. I use a floating line on my Spey rod and a leader the length of the rod. There are a lot of places to wade and there are a lot of lies that are waist deep that are perfect for fly-fishing. But it's tough fishing. The water is real clear, and the fish can be real tough. You can see them but it doesn't mean you are going to catch them."

Perhaps more than on any other West End river, there is a stark distinction between the Calawah's two forks. This is partially the result of the difference in ownership, with the South Fork above Sitkum River having enjoyed the protection of Olympic National Park since the 1930s, while the North Fork flows through a mixture of National Forest and private land. However, the greatest single factor in the current state of the North Fork of the Calawah was the 1951 Forks Fire. Originating on the Sol Duc near the Olympic National Park boundary, the fire burned 30,000 acres, two-thirds of the watershed, in two days. It has been identified as the largest fire in that area since 1100 A.D. After the ashes cooled, salvage logging began.

Even more than the Sol Duc, the upper river is a dangerous place for a boater, and the reach above the forks shouldn't be attempted under any circumstances. It isn't exactly a cakewalk downstream, either, although the WDFW built a fancy new boat ramp on the mainstem just north of Forks. Experienced guides who know the river intimately warned repeatedly that the section from the ramp down to the mouth was too rough for amateurs, and sure enough several boats were destroyed the first winter the launch was open. A much better approach for a newcomer is to fish with a guide or on foot. As on the Sol Duc, there are plenty of gated roads and a mixture of Department of Natural Resources, Forest Service and private timberlands. The best time to prospect it is during spring, when the river is dropping and warming, and the last pulse of big bright fish is moving up from the Bogachiel.

"This is just my opinion but I think steelhead revert back to more trout-like behavior when the water temperature gets above 45 degrees and the nymphs begin moving around," veteran West End steelhead guide Herb Jacobsen said. "As the insect activity picks up on the rivers, I start using larger, more buggy patterns. In April, I also fish a lot of surface or subsurface flies on floating line, even on a greased line. You can use a little spider or marabou fly-fished greased line. I like black with a green butt of peacock or ostrich."

Chapter Twenty-three

Refugia

I don't spend as much time on West End rivers during the early part of the winter as I did a decade or two ago. I still make a few trips in late November and early December, before the bulk of the hatchery fish make an appearance, but most of my effort now occurs after mid-January. This isn't indicative of any flagging interest or cooling passions as I turn into an old man. Nor is it really a response to the dramatic increase in crowding on the rivers, because most of the places I fish aren't heavily fished by out-of-towners, anyway. No, the main reason you won't find me on my favorite rivers in early winter is that I am duck hunting. My extremely intense and talented, yet episodically cooperative, yellow Labrador retriever, Lily, and I hunted 75 days between early October and mid-January last year.

"My fly rods don't care if I take them fishing," is the way I explain this to friends. "But my dog cares if I don't take her hunting."

Lily and I hunt the salt marsh and sloughs behind our home on northern Hood Canal. During the early season, resident mallards, which I avoid shooting because I have watched them all summer, and green-wing teal, which I have a hard time hitting, are the birds we see most. By early November, though, migratory birds—widgeon, "northern" mallards, and pintails—make an appearance. Nearly all of these ducks hatched far to the north, on public lands in Alberta, British Columbia or Alaska, or on land purchased and protected by Ducks Unlimited. Enough of them, especially widgeon, winter in the area to keep Lily and me busy, but the majority eventually move on down the coast to the scattered islands of National Wildlife Refuges to the south—Lewis and Clark, at the mouth of the Columbia, to Klamath and Tule Lake—and into Mexico.

President Theodore Roosevelt is usually credited with establishing the system of National Wildlife Refuges when he designated Pelican Island in Florida as a sanctuary for egrets, spoonbills and herons from the plume hunters in 1903. Since then, more than 500 federal refuges have been established, and they preserve 92 million acres of critical upland and wetland habitat from the Arctic tundra to the Florida Keys and from the prairie potholes to the New Mexico desert. Most of the refuges were initially set aside to preserve migratory waterfowl habitat, and today more than 100 million ducks and geese nest or winter on the refuges. In addition to the government refuges, Ducks Unlimited has purchased thousands of additional acres in Canada and the United States as sanctuaries for nesting waterfowl.

But President Benjamin Harrision actually established an earlier federal refuge in 1892, and it was created to protect salmon and forests, not birds. The Afognak Salmon and Forest Reserve closed all commercial and subsistence fishing and prohibited development around Alaska's Afognak Island and in its Uganick River. The person behind the nation's first "salmon park" was Livingstone Stone, a retired Unitarian minister and member of the U.S. Fish Commission. Stone had witnessed first-hand the decline of Atlantic salmon on East Coast streams, and he had become alarmed over pressures on Pacific salmon in the Northwest. "If we procrastinate and put off our rescuing mission too long, it may be too late to do any good," he told the 1892 meeting of the American Fisheries Society. "After the rivers are ruined and the salmon gone they cannot be reclaimed."

Stone's idea, of course, occurred at precisely the moment when hatcheries emerged as the great panacea for dwindling fish runs. Indeed, Stone was a fish culture advocate himself, having built the first anadromous fish hatchery on the West Coast in 1872, and one of the motivations behind the Afognak refuge was to protect the water supply for a hatchery. Over subsequent decades, as Afognak was gradually stripped of its protection, the concept of establishing protected habitat for salmon was discarded, and hatcheries became the principle tool of Pacific Coast fish managers. Today, there are more than 80 major steelhead hatcheries, as well as scores of additional salmon and trout hatcheries. Even the U.S. Fish and Wildlife Service, the agency charged with administering the nation's wildlife refuges, paradoxically, operates 11 salmon and steelhead hatcheries on the West Coast, including the Quinault, Quilcene and Makah hatcheries on the Olympic Peninsula. Afognak Island was the first and last "salmon park."

A century after Afognak, the differences between the status of native waterfowl and wild steelhead in the Pacific Northwest are dramatic and telling. When Lily and I hunt the marsh behind our house, we pursue wild ducks and we kill them. So do hunters at Potholes Reservoir and Malheur Lake, at Skagit Bay and Klamath Lake. There are no such things as hatchery ducks and "catch-and-release" is, well, absurd on its face. Yet ducks are fairly abundant in most areas, the seasons are long and the bag limits are generous. On the other hand, most steelhead populations in the Pacific Northwest today are listed as endangered species or are candidates for listing. Wild release is required in nearly all areas except the Olympic Peninsula. Despite the continuing expenditures of hundreds of millions of dollars, hatchery returns are unpredictable, and they provide short seasons and small bag limits.

Perhaps not surprisingly, as steelhead and salmon population have collapsed, there has been a revival of interest in salmonid sanctuaries. It has become obvious that the rivers that have maintained strong populations of wild anadromous fish virtually always lie within protected areas—national parks, federally-protected wilderness or wild and scenic rivers. The feature all of these varied systems share are extensive unbroken reaches of unaltered habitat. It has also become increasingly clear that protecting productive fish habitat is not only more effective than restoring degraded habitat, it is also usually cheaper.

"In the 107 years since Livingstone Stone called for the establishment of salmon parks," Lichatowich, Rahr, Whidden and Steward wrote in "Sanctuaries for Pacific Salmon," "the need for salmon refuges has grown stronger. Yet our ability to establish true refuges for native salmon has diminished. The remaining productive habitat is disappearing rapidly. However, no factor is as important to the persistence of wild salmonids as the presence of good habitat for spawning, rearing, cover and migration."

Of all the advocates of salmon refugia, none has staked out a more ambitious terrain than the Oregon-based Wild Salmon Center. Best known for its efforts to preserve entire anadromous fish systems, even entire regions, in Russia's pristine Kamchatka region, the Wild Salmon Center's Cascadia Project has also identified Pacific Northwest rivers that deserve permanent protection. "In some of the upper parts of these watersheds, salmon refugia are on public lands, and are already protected from major human disturbance," it explained in its 1999 report. "However, on the lower sections of almost all of these watersheds, where the most productive habitats were historically located, there is no habitat protection." On the Olympic Peninsula, it selected the middle and lower Hoh River, and in 2002, it acquired 850 acres at Schmidt Bar, near the mouth of Elk Creek.

The Hoh was a logical choice. It still supports strong populations of wild migratory salmonids, including species such as steelhead, spring chinook and bull trout that have been reduced dramatically in other areas of the Northwest. More than 65 percent of the basin lies within the boundaries of Olympic National Park, which ensures its headwaters will continue to function properly. Yet much of the watershed's low-elevation spawning and nursery habitat is currently owned by timber companies or the Washington Department of Natural Resources and is subject to timber harvest. Unlike the other rainforest rivers, where the overwhelming bulk of riparian land is held by the federal and tribal governments, there is land in the Hoh that can be purchased and dedicated to other uses.

"Our goal is to protect the best of the best," said John McMillan, the Cascadia Program's Olympic Peninsula representative. "The Hoh has probably the best habitat remaining in the lower 48 states. Our goal is to provide a sanctuary out here."

Before signing on with the Wild Salmon Center, John was a fish biologist with the Hoh Indian Tribe. He regularly snorkels steelhead and salmon rivers, and has hiked virtually all of the tributaries. One of the things his research has documented is the importance of habitat outside the national park. Indeed, although the vast majority of spring/summer chinook spawn within the park, upwards of 70 percent of fall chinook and more than 50 percent of the coho redds occur downstream of the park boundary. Similarly, less than 20 percent of the redds of tributary spawning winter steelhead were identified in the park. The remainder (71 percent of the total) were overwhelmingly from the handful of tributaries that flow into the mainstem between Highway 101 and the national park boundary.

John has identified the concentration of creek mouths and floodplains above the Hoh Oxbow as one of the basin's most productive areas, and it is where the Wild Salmon Center will concentrate its efforts. It is the site of the Schmidt Bar acquisition, and is also where Winflield, Elk, Alder and Willoughby creeks flow into the Hoh. "They all flow into the mainstem in the five miles or so above the Hoh Oxbow," John said. "That area has the widest flood plain in the whole basin. The largest portions of Winfield and Elk creeks flow over glacial terraces. Elk Creek was the most stable. It was the best of the best. But we want a well-dispersed network. We don't want to put all of our eggs in one basket." The Wild Salmon Center has also identified Nolan Creek, Owl Creek and the South Fork of the Hoh as important candidates for refugia status, as well as the floodplain complexes along Braden, Anderson, Pins and Clear creeks.

You can't get much of an indication of why the reach above the oxbow is so productive from a road map, but the U.S. Geological Survey 7.5 minute Winfield Creek and Spruce Mountain topographical maps reveal many of the features that make it so worthy of added protection. Rising up on the steep north slope that divides the Hoh from the Bogachiel, where the contour lines are close together on the map, the blue line representing Alder Creek drops quickly to a large, low-elevation floodplain. The contour lines spread even farther apart on the opposite side of the river, along lower Winfield and Elk creeks, and the low-gradient river bottoms extend more than two miles away from the river. To the east, Owl Creek, which was the basin's most productive chinook tributary until the infamous debris flows of November 1990, heads up on the back side of Heulsdonk Ridge, then bends around to the north and meanders across a series of low-gradient forested terraces before flowing into the mainstem near the old Heulsdonk homestead.

Maps are fun on a winter evening, especially when you've got a nice fire crackling and the rain is hammering the windowpanes, but it's a lot more interesting to pull on a pair of waterproof hiking boots and explore these creek mouths and terraces. One of the first things you will notice is the extraordinary amount of water that is not within the main channel. There are feeder creeks that flow into tributaries and hillside seeps and relict side channels and forested wetlands and crystal-clear ponds. Water seems to be virtually everywhere in the Hoh River floodplain, which probably isn't that surprising in a rain forest. But some of the watershed's most important water, water that the Wild Salmon Center is determined to protect, is not visible. It is the groundwater and the water within the hyporheic zone, the saturated area of gravel between the river channel bottom and the groundwater.

"A lot of people think that the Hoh is so cold because of its glaciers," John said. "But glacial influence has little to do with it." He explained that the thing that keeps it so cold is its gravel outwash, which allows a complex set of interactions between the water in the river's channel and its alluvial aquifer. As a result, the water in the Hoh and other rainforest rivers maintains a nearly constant temperature year round. "The Hoh almost never gets below 35 degrees Fahrenheit in winter and it is usually in the 40- to 60-degree range. That compares with the Sol Duc, where the temperature is around 35 degrees or lower in cold weather, and it ranges up to 72 degrees." Unlike the gravel, the large boulders and bedrock on the Sol Duc hold the heat.

Additionally, recent investigations of the hyporheic zone have revealed previously unimagined complexity within gravel outwash river systems such as the Hoh. Much of this work has been conducted at the Flathead Lake Research Station by Jack Stanford, a scientific advisor with the Wild Salmon Center and a mentor of John McMillan. Stanford's and others' research has shown that the hyporheic zones in low-gradient valley floor areas similar to the middle reach of the Hoh can be significantly larger than the main channel. Indeed, hyporheic zones with depths in excess of 600 meters and lateral reaches of between three and five kilometers have been discovered.

"They are finding that water may remain in the zone for three or four years," John said, "and up to 95 percent of the biomass of a river is produced in the alluvial aquifer. Fish, usually coho and probably some juvenile steelhead, can go down and pass through the aquifer, through the interstitial spaces in the gravel. They have found amazing animals—blind snakes and frogs." Insects are also abundant within the zone, including species familiar to fly-fishers such as net-spinning *Hydropsyche* caddisflies and a variety of stoneflies. "It is a marvelous thing, really." However, there are concerns that increased sediment loads from headwater tributaries could reduce the productivity of the aquifer and hyporheic zone. "Could we plug it?" John wondered.

If the Hoh's freshwater ecosystem is a remarkable, yet threatened, resource, then so are its trees, especially the large trees that end up in the river. "We need wood," John said. "It's the key factor out here. Wood is a limiting factor for fish. You can't go wrong with wood and it has to be big wood." John's research has shown that wood density is strongly correlated to 79 percent of the steelhead, 83 percent of the coho and 75 percent of the cutthroat juveniles in tributaries. And he says that the Sitka spruce, the dominant conifer of the Olympic Peninsula's rain forests, is the best tree to create complex fish habitat. "The spruce is the perfect tree," he said. "Its root wad is flat—big and broad and flat." This creates vertical, in addition to downstream, flow and more variation in temperature for the fish. "We also need big rocks or wood to keep the pathways to the ground water open," he observed, "Otherwise they can become encrusted with silt and fines."

Unlike most of the biologists I have known, John is comfortable with metaphor and employs it gracefully and creatively. "Protecting the headwaters of a river is analogous to protecting the nesting areas of ducks in Alberta," he said, as we spoke in his home office in Forks. The headwaters of the Hoh are already a refugia in Olympic National Park. "If you look at Mexico where the ducks winter, it is like the ocean or the estuary," he said. The Hoh Tribe and Olympic National Park control most of the Hoh estuary. "Then in between them you have the flyways," said. "They are akin to the mainstem migratory routes of the fish that you've got to protect."

Those migratory pathways and the processes that support them are what John and the Wild Salmon Center are trying to protect on the Hoh and, with any luck, on other West End rivers in the future.

Chapter Twenty-four

Elwha

Although it falls outside the area commonly referred to as the West End, the Elwha River always comes up sooner or later when you talk about winter steelhead with veteran Olympic Peninsula anglers. The story of the Elwha and its anadromous fish is well known to virtually all Northwesterners. Originally one of the region's most productive migratory fish systems, the Elwha historically hosted all five species of Northwest salmon, including a strain of chinook that produced documented 100-plus-pound fish. But the river and its fisheries have been in steady decline since two dams without fish passage were built on the lower river in the early 1900s. Now, after decades of wrangling, there is a chance that the Elwha and Glines Canyon dams might be removed within the next few years, and anadromous fish might once again swim deep into the Elwha backcountry.

"The Elwha was the best river on the Olympic Peninsula," Dick Goin recalled. "It was impossible to beat the Elwha. I remember a day over 50 years ago when I caught 18 steelhead on a bamboo fly rod on bait and flies. That was unusual, but it was very common to have a 10-fish day. That was common way into the mid and late 1950s. It had the best, the scrappiest steelhead. They did honest-to-God tailwalking. It was common. The first winter runs showed up between November 5 and 10. They were like northern fish. They would jump 15 times. Thirty years after the dams, it seemed the Elwha still had way more fish than the other rivers. But when I talked to older guys they always said, 'It's not much compared to the older days.'"

Even though it flows into the Strait of Juan de Fuca near the center of the peninsula, the Elwha shares intimate connections with the large West End rivers. It rises up deep within the mountainous backcountry of Olympic National Park, on snowfields and glaciers not much more than a rifle shot from the upper fingers of the Queets and Hoh. The Elwha is, similarly, only separated from the upper North Fork of the Quinault River by Low Divide, the lowest backcountry pass in the Olympics. Like the major coastal rivers, it is a large system, the fourth-largest on the peninsula, draining more than 321 square miles on its 45-mile course. It is also similar to the Quillayute and rainforest rivers in that it hosted a complex system of anadromous salmonids before the dams, with fish returning every month of the year and occupying virtually every habitat niche.

"We fished for kings too, you know," Dick said. "They were jumpers, even the big ones. Forty-pounders were common and we hooked fish fairly regularly that were scary. Cohos were all over the place. The resident trout in the canyons were so rich even in the presence of anadromy. They ranged up to three or four pounds, with an occasional fish to six pounds. They were very responsive to a dry fly. There was so much food down in the canyons—eggs and fry and crayfish and insects, incredible caddis hatches. During the summer there would be all kinds of fish around the bridge. They had a sort of pecking order, with resident trout and sea-run cutthroat and resident and migratory Dollies. There would be half-pounder and adult steelhead mixed in. The first one hooked would always be an adult summer steelhead."

Despite its similarities to the West End rivers, the Elwha is unique. After an original course to the southeast, it quickly buttonhooks to the north, the only major Olympic Peninsula river other than the Dungeness to flow north. It absorbs a number of significant tributaries—Godkin Creek, Hayes River, the Goldie, Lost River—but it lacks the headwater "forks" that are characteristic of many coastal rivers. More than any other Olympic Peninsula river, the Elwha is also a river of mountains. While the lowlands of the Quillayute and rainforest rivers extend through foothills for miles before climbing into the high country, the Elwha enters the mountains within a dozen miles of the strait. As with the Quinault, its course leeward of the Bailey Range results in less precipitation than West End rivers, and it floods less frequently.

It is hard today to truly imagine the bounty of the Elwha before the dams, but the historical record contains tantalizing, even occasionally mysterious, glimpses. On March 26, 1890, Press Expedition leader, James Christie, fished the Geyeser Valley section of the Elwha, a short distance above Goblin's Gate. "Then followed one-half hour of as fine fishing as any I ever enjoyed on the thousand streams I have had the pleasure fishing in," he wrote in his journal, "carrying to camp fourteen splendid trout; weight about forty pounds; no mean basket from any water." According to Captain Charles Barnes journal, which corroborates Christie's description of the fish, these "most delicious salmon trout" ranged from 22 to 26 inches in length.

What species of fish were these? I have wondered about that many times. They couldn't have been salmon, because salmon die after spawning in the fall or winter, and they were too small to be early-returning spring chinook. They were rather tightly grouped and of a peculiarly uniform and small size for winter steelhead, as well. I have encountered thick schools of native char on rainforest rivers in the past, and the upper Elwha supports a good population of char today. The size also seems about right for char, and the timing suggests they could have been either resident fish or anadromous char on their way downstream. But Dick Goin says the Elwha historically hosted a run of small "half-pounder" summer steelhead, and I have wondered if they could have been half-pounders on their way back downstream after wintering in the upper river? Or one-salt summer steelhead kelts?

Today, the Elwha currently only sees winter steelhead returns around one-tenth of the Quillayute System rivers. In 1992, after three-quarters of a century of dwindling fish runs—including the virtual extirpation of the Elwha's legendary spring chinook, pink and sockeye salmon—Congress passed the Elwha River Eco system and Fisheries Restoration Act. It authorized the removal of the lower Elwha and upper Glines Canyon dams. Successive Republican Congresses, led by Washington Senator Slade Gorton refused to fully fund the act, however, and in 1998 Elwha chinook and chum salmon were listed as endangered species. The Clinton administration finally secured the appropriations to purchase the two dams, and currently engineering and decommissioning studies are underway. The lower Elwha Dam may come down within the next few years.

The reason anglers and the Lower Elwha S'Klallam Tribe have struggled so long and so tenaciously to remove the dams is simple—habitat. The lower Elwha, the five miles of river below the

Elwha Dam, is virtually bereft of productive spawning gravel or stable nursery areas, and the section of river between Lake Aldwell and the Olympic National Park boundary contains relatively poor habitat, as well. But upstream of Glines Canyon Dam, which accounts for more than 70 percent of the drainage, the Elwha is an essentially pristine ecosystem. It lies not only within Olympic National Park; but also in roadless wilderness in Olympic National Park. In essence, the entire 220-plus square miles of the basin above Lake Mills has functioned as a salmon habitat preserve for the last 85 years.

"Given the available high-quality habitat in Olympic National Park," McHenry, Lichatowich and Kowalki-Hagamann wrote in "Status of Salmon and Their Habitats on the Olympic Peninsula, Washington," "the authors feel that removal of the dams on the Elwha River remains the best and most cost-effective opportunity for salmon restoration on the Olympic Peninsula, and possibly the western United States."

The ecological and economic coherence behind Elwha restoration is compelling for anyone who has ever been involved with traditional salmonid restoration. These projects always follow a virtually identical narrative: A private interest makes a profit from the exploitation of a natural resource, either public or private, then the taxpayer is required to contribute money to "restore" the resource to a fraction of its productivity. Attempts to curtail further habitat degradation on a meaningful scale are denounced as restricting "economic growth." Growth is necessary for jobs and the tax base and even schools, we are told by county commissioners and realtors and the chambers of commerce, and growth means trophy homes and shopping centers, gravel mines and trailer parks. Much like a wildfire, economic growth needs constant fuel, and the fuel it feeds upon is fish, waterfowl and wildlife habitat. Increasingly, the oxygen that nourishes the wildfire is supplied by the salmon restoration industry.

"Habitat restoration is intensely political," Dick Goin said. "There are rivers that are not repairable. Salmon restoration is a hollow, hollow phrase. Look at a truly wild river. The Queets is a truly wild river. Then compare it with a channelized and degraded river. It is not within our grasp to restore all rivers. Even with the best of intentions, we can't restore but a fragment of these rivers."

But the situation on the Elwha could not be more different. Indeed, the recovery of Elwha steelhead and salmon is less about restoration than it is about salmonid liberation. The point of removing the dams, after all, is to provide the fish access to the three-quarters of the watershed that needs no restoration because it is pristine. Public funds will be spent to acquire and dismantle the dams, to draw down the reservoirs and to re-introduce salmonids, but with the exception of limited hatchery outplanting to re-seed the river, human activity should conclude in a relatively short time. Then it will be up to the fish. If harvest is controlled in the lower river and ocean, the steelhead and salmon will re-establish themselves, exactly as they have done after floods and fires and earthquakes and, most recently, in the rivers that drain Mount St. Helens, volcanoes for thousands of years.

The fish that spawned lower in the system—especially the sockeye that swam up Indian Creek to Lake Sutherland and the pink and chum that spawned in the lower 16 miles of the Elwha—will be hardest to re-establish. The habitat they used is most abused, and it will experience the flow of accumulated silt after the dams are removed. But the spring and summer chinook, the anadromous char, the coho, and the winter and summer steelhead that swam far into the Elwha backcountry have excellent chances of becoming self-sustaining with minimal human intervention. Of all the species, steelhead should be the easiest to recover, because, unlike the backcountry salmon, which died out within a life cycle of the completion of the lower dam, the descendants of wild winter steelhead still swim in the upper river.

"The genetic analysis indicated that the fish of the upper river were not closely related to hatchery fish and grouped more closely with wild coastal winter steelhead," said John Meyer, Olympic National Park head fisheries biologist. "We hope to use the fish as broodstock for re-introducing steelhead to the upper river if the dams are removed."

The reinvention of steelhead fishing on the upper Elwha won't be without struggles, exasperating, enervating struggles if past experiences are any indication. The proximity of the river to Port Angeles will almost certainly result in intense pressure to open a sport fishery as soon as possible, probably long before it is biologically responsible. Once fishing resumes, there will doubtlessly be concerted efforts, most likely from the WDFW and politicians like Jim Buck, to allow wild harvest and to flood the middle and lower river with hatchery fish. As the average age of the population continues to rise—and the median age on the Olympic Peninsula is already considerably older than the rest of the country—there will also probably be moves to "open up" the backcountry, to allow ATVs, or shuttles or snowmobiles to transport those not fit enough for trails.

Having come this far, though, it is impossible not to imagine the days that lie ahead. It may not all come together while my knees and lungs can still handle the trail, but my stepson, Morgan, will almost certainly eventually slip a backpack from his shoulders after the long hike from Whiskey Bend to Elkhorn Ranger Station. That is where the Elwha River Trail drops back down to the river after the long traverse above the Grand Canyon of the Elwha. Summer steelhead will hold in the flats and riffles there, perhaps all the way upstream to Camp Wilder and Godkin Creek. When the snow and blowdown block the trail into the upper river, he will stick to the glides above Goblin's Gate, to the riffles in Krause Bottom and the mouth of Long River. He will see the elk that have always wintered in the bottoms there, along with the bears in spring. And for the first time in generations, he will cast for the thick-shouldered steelhead of winter, those charcoal, silver and pearl emissaries from the sea.

Chapter Twenty-five
Calypso Orchids

It was a beautiful April day, with a flawless blue sky, temperatures that would climb into the low 60s and a soft breeze that carried the scent of elderberry blossoms. Most of the West End rivers were closed. The Hoh and Queets rivers had closed a couple of weeks earlier, the Hoko at the end of March, and the smaller rivers like the Pysht and Goodman Creek had been closed since the end of February. But you could still fish in Quillayute system tributaries, the Sol Duc, Bogachiel, Dickey and Calawah, and I had heard that a pulse of fresh fish had been pulled into the Sol Duc by a recent storm. Even better, the focus of effort of many anglers had switched to lakes, something I never understand when steelhead are available, but I certainly take advantage of it.

I was in a bad mood, though. It had taken me longer than I wanted to assemble all of my gear and lunch and to get on the road. The traffic on Highway 101 had stoked my crankiness. As recently as a decade ago, it was possible to drive between Discovery Bay and Port Angeles in the predawn hours without seeing more than a handful of vehicles, but that day huge trucks and SUVs were on my bumper the minute I passed Fat Schmitty's Restuarant. I had no idea where all of these people were going at 5:30 in the morning, but they were definitely in a hurry and already had a full head of aggression. Probably something to do with real estate or development, I thought, sourly. The news on the radio was pretty grim, too.

I was also, frankly, still annoyed by an article I had read the night before. It was yet another profile of winter steelhead fly-fishing on the Olympic Peninsula. It was a virtual exemplar of the style I refer to as the "White Hunter" school of outdoor writing. This term refers to the articles I used to read in the national outdoor magazines as a kid, where well-heeled old men traveled to Africa or India and shot big game. This genre has, for the most part, mercifully vanished, but the psychological impetus behind it seems, lamentably, to have been transferred virtually full blown into a segment of fly-fishing. It is manifested by writers who sweep into areas, talk to a couple of fly shop employees, fish with a guide for a day or two, then produce a lavishly illustrated article or guide book. The most laughably galling example of this approach to outdoor writing occurred in a book I read that said the Hoh and the Sol Duc were "similar."

Fortunately, the Olympic Peninsula still abounds with sights and sounds and seasonal rhythms that are utterly overlooked by the authors of these "consumer reports" style articles, but that anchor a local resident firmly in place. I saw one of my favorite springtime sights on the eastern outskirts of Port Angeles that morning, one that has marked the passage of seasons for me on my way to West End steelhead rivers for many years. Each April, the new foliage on the trees above Morse Creek create a delicate mosaic of green. The big leaf maple catkins are a yellowish-green, the new leaves on the alders are darker green, and the fir trees above the creek are an even darker, blacker green. Seeing it that day soothed my discomfiture like a balm.

I passed through P.A. quickly, and after the junction with Highway 112—the road to Neah Bay—the traffic pretty much vanished. I caught a glimpse of the heavy mantle of snow on Mount Carrie on the steep grade down to the Elwha, then glanced at my old cabin as I crossed the Elwha River bridge. I had begun to relax, to breathe more deeply, more slowly. I stopped at the Shadow Mountain Resort, west of Lake Sutherland, and bought a cup of coffee. I drove a few more miles and pulled off at a turnout on Lake Crescent and drank my coffee. By the time I swung off the highway and bounced down the two-track toward the Sol Duc, I felt like an entirely different person. I took my time getting into waders and vest and assembling my Spey rod. Then I followed a faint trail into the woods.

I hadn't walked more than five minutes when I heard the hollow rapping of a woodpecker. It took me a minute to locate it, but I eventually saw the bird, a pileated woodpecker. I marveled as always at its exotic, almost Aztec-looking, plumage. The forest was primarily western hemlock and Douglas fir, with a chaotic litter of blowdown and thick carpet of organic matter. This area was part of the calamitous 1951 Fork Fire, but I think most of the downed trees are of more recent vintage, maybe from the famous 1960 Columbus Day storm. Pink buds had emerged on the red huckleberry bushes in the open patches. I had picked berries from these bushes many times during the summer. I recognized the spots under the oldest, most moldering blowdown where I would find chanterelle mushrooms in the fall.

Over the last twenty years, I have fished many of the reaches of the large and small West End rivers. I have also floated most of them in drift boats. But I find myself concentrating more and more on a handful of locations for winter steelhead. This isn't the case during summer, when I wander all over the place in search of cutthroat, but during the winter I seem to have refined my angling down to a few choice spots on each river. There is a hole on the Hoh that I fish as much as any. If I had to restrict myself to just one piece of water, I would pick it without hesitation. But the Hoh is blown out a lot, so it is a good thing that the Sol Duc isn't really that "similar" to the Hoh. Otherwise, I would miss a lot of fishing over the course of a year. I also have sweet spots on the Queets and South Fork Calawah, Pysht and Hoko and Bogachiel. I still like to explore new water, but these holes and drifts and slots are like the books and records I have carried around for decades. They are not only places of affection, they are the fabric of my life.

This Sol Duc River tailout is one of those places. Located between two long, high-gradient rapids, it features a relatively flat glide that narrows into a broad pool and boulder-strewn tailout. It is a great place to swing a fly, either with a Spey rod from the bank or, when the river is lower, from upstream. It is also one of those places where the conventional wisdom about how to fish steelhead occasionally works. When the water is high, fish tend to cluster along the broken water and rocks below the tailout, while they are usually in the apron of slick water just downstream of the rapids when the water is low. You never really know, though, so it is important to fish it all thoroughly. It is also a good place to fish in spring, because steelhead hold there after the rough water downstream but don't seem to spawn, maybe because there is a lot of sand on the bottom.

There were no footprints on the sand, only an old rain-spattered cougar track. The upper Sol Duc was also way too low for a drift boat. I knew that any fish that were present wouldn't have seen a line, at least not so far today. It was with a rising, buoyant sense of anticipation, then, that I tied on a Syd Glass pattern, an Orange Heron. I had bartered it from a friend for a couple of widgeon skins. I began with roll casts from the bank, fishing the edges of the shallow flat next to shore, then waded out to the head of run. With the added reach of my 14-foot rod, I was able to work the sink-tip about 60 feet away. I drew it slowly across the break where the moving water and softer water of the pool meet.

Suddenly, I noticed an eagle. It was a mature bald eagle and it landed atop a fir snag on the far bank. The sight of the bird took me involuntarily back to an incident that occurred more than a decade earlier. I had been on my way to fish this exact spot when I was startled by a commotion near the river. It was an eagle on the ground among the ferns. It squawked and hopped a few feet when it saw me. I stopped abruptly, aware that it was odd that the eagle hadn't flown away. Then the fish flopped. It was a steelhead, a 12- or 14-pound fish. It flopped again, and I saw that one of its eyes had been plucked out. It was still fairly bright, with just a faint blush of red along its lateral line and gill plates. It was a hen.

"Get out of here," I yelled instinctively at the bird.

It flapped up to a streamside tree, landing on a broken-off limb 50 feet above the ground. The steelhead flopped again, and I could see that both ot its eyes were gone. I walked over to the fish. Other than its eyes, there wasn't any visible damage. Its belly was still heavy with eggs. Without thinking about it, I picked it up and carried it to the edge of the river. I looked back up at the eagle, who was glaring down at me balefully. I bent over and eased the steelhead into the river. It was still strong, and I could feel its rippling liquid muscles. It shook itself briefly, almost a shudder, then swam downstream.

I have regretted that impulsive act for a decade. As someone who rails ceaselessly against managers and agencies that think they know how to control the lives of fish and wildlife better than the animals do, it was certainly hypocritical. I turned myself into a God from the Machine. My motivations were benign—I wanted the steelhead to spawn, or at least not be pecked to death while it was still relatively strong, but it was toweringly stupid and arrogant to intervene. It also suggested that I, too, have created a hierarchy of animals, one in which steelhead trump eagles. For all I know, it may even have been illegal. More practically, the fish probably just floated a few hundred yards downstream and was eaten by something else, maybe even the same eagle. I hope so.

Now, ten years later, I wondered if the eagle above me could be the same one. It watched me for a while as I fished the run. Then it flew downstream, no doubt looking for a spawned-out steelhead. By now, I had covered everything from the head of the pool down through the edge of the rock garden above the rapids. I could have tied on a different fly, a General Practitioner or stonefly nymph, and fished the water again, but this was probably my last winter steelhead trip of the season, and there were two other lies upstream that I wanted to hit. Wading out of the river, I sat down on a large, moss-covered rock and ate half of my ham sandwich.

On my way back to the car, I detoured off the path a short distance. I crawled over a couple of blowdown hemlock to a small opening. Shafts of sunlight broke through the gap in the canopy made by the fallen trees. It was nearly mid-day now. The ground smelled warm and rich. It was covered with a spongy blanket of moss and conifer needles. I slowed down and began carefully scanning the forest floor. I didn't see anything but needles and salal and duff for a moment, but then my eyes picked up a flash of purple. It was a Calypso orchid, just what I had been looking for. Over the next few minutes, I discovered a half-dozen more of the delicate, nodding pale violet forest flowers.

Calypso orchids, also known as fairy slippers, are one of the Northwest's most beautiful flowers, and one of the rarest. Their scientific name, ***Calypso bulbosa***, is a reference to the seductive woodland nymph in Greek mythology who kept Odysseus on her island for seven years on his way home from the Trojan War. Calypso orchids only occur in areas rich in organic matter, and their natural low abundance has been significantly reduced as a result of human activity. The plant's above-ground stems and leaf are only connected to the corm by fragile threadlike roots, and when the flowers are picked the plant invariably dies. Unlike most flowering plants, Calypso orchids do not produce enough chlorophyll to survive. They, instead, tap nutrients from the fungus beneath the soil known as the mycorhizal layer. Botanists have only begun to understand the interactions between the mycorhizal layer and the orchids, but it is a delicate and intricate relationship.

It doesn't take a lot of imagination to make a connection between wild winter steelhead and Calypso orchids. Both are unaccountably lovely. Both are elusive. The literal translation of Calypso is, in fact, "concealer." And they both thrive in the same places—the dark, moist forests of the north Pacific slope. Like my favorite winter steelhead holes, they are also only found in very specific sites within much larger areas that appear identical. In the century and a half since Euro-Americans began the transformation of the Northwest landscape, they have also both declined precipitately. There are differences between the two species. The disappearance of orchids has gone largely unremarked upon, while the decline of steelhead has set in motion a virtual juggernaut of restoration, advocacy and legislation. But the fate of both remains uncertain.

One thing is certain, though, and that is that we still really don't know a damned thing about many of the processes or relationships that sustain the unique ecologies of the Olympic Peninsula. On the Hoh and Queets, the North Fork of the Calawah and Quinault, scientists are only beginning to understand the functions of the hyporheic zone. It has only been a handful of years, as well, since the dynamics of tides and creeks within estuaries have even begun to be examined. Within the forests, especially the rainforest valleys, it is only a couple of decades since botanists discovered that the lush tapestries of mosses and epiphytes in the forest canopy are not simply benign but that the giant trees absorb nutrients from them. And down on the forest floor, 300 feet below in some cases, the investigations into the relationships between the mycohrizal zone and Calypso orchids have barely scratched the surface.

There is still much about West End steelhead that is yet to be understood, as well. "One of the exciting things about these fish is there is still a lot to be learned," J.D. Love told me. "I've fished these rivers for 30 years and there are sections of streams five miles from here that I haven't fished. We are just beginning to learn about the resident rainbows. It's also great when you can catch a winter steelhead in October or summer steelhead in March. It's great to live on a river system where you can still be surprised, where the fish are healthy enough to exhibit eccentric parts of their life histories."

Jack Ward Thomas, the first wildlife biologist to head the Forest Service, put it eloquently: "Not only are ecosystems more complex than we think, they are more complex than we can think."

In the face of such uncertainties, a cautious, even humble, approach to managing fish would seem to be in order. The wild winter steelhead of the West End of the Olympic Peninsula are, after all, the last reasonably healthy regional complex of winter steelhead in the lower 48 states. But it isn't happening. The State of Washington has, instead, gambled the wild steelhead of the Sol Duc and Deep Creek, the Dickey and the Queets, the Hoh and Mosquito Creek in a last-ditch defense of the two most discredited artifacts of 20th century fisheries management—Chambers Creek hatchery steelhead and maximum sustained harvest. Indeed, the WDFW's current management of these rivers seems driven entirely by a desperate urge to curry political favor and sell licenses. Rather than humble and cautious, the words reckless and arrogant come to mind.

"All of the biologists I talk with in the field have always been dedicated and hard working and willing to lay things on the line," Jim Lichatowich told me when we discussed *Salmon Without Rivers*. "When you move from the field to the desks, though, you run into politics. Then the difference between the good guys and the bad guys gets murky. If you look at the bulk of the people in agencies, they are doing an excellent job generally. But they don't get support from the upper management and administrative levels."

I read a gorgeous sentiment in one of Barry Lopez's books recently,"True understanding of an area comes not so much from an encyclopedic knowledge," he said. "It comes rather from intimacy."

That describes the exact opposite ethos of that demonstrated by the "biocrats," to use J.D. Love's term, in Olympia and Portland and Seattle. It is also intrinsically contrary to the motivations behind the "White Hunters" that I mentioned earlier. On the Olympic Peninsula, it is the knowledge of West End loggers, who know where the steelhead lie and where the 6X6 bull elk is on opening day. It is the wisdom of habitat biologists, who work the watersheds on a daily basis. It is also the knowledge of anglers who have spent lifetimes on these rivers and have seen them after fires, in flood and in drought, and at times of extraordinary abundance. It is the knowledge that eventually ripens into wisdom.

That takes time, of course, time that is measured in decades not in days. But the rewards are profound, whether an angler's home water is a West End river, an urban seashore or a chain of lakes. Because at the end of twenty or thirty years, you have a connection to the water that the White Hunters, with their frantic scrambles to notch all the famous destinations on their rod handles, can never even begin to comprehend. You also develop your own idiosyncratic natural history of the area, one that is illuminated by your own stories and secrets and ways to observe the passage of the years. If you are lucky enough to have become besotted of the water that is close to where you live, you will also inevitably come to feel strongly protective of its fish and the habitat that supports it.

"We lived down on the Elwha," Dick Goin explained to me when I asked him how he could stand to attend so many meetings about salmon restoration and habitat protection. "Our protein source was salmon. They basically sustained us for a long time. I feel it's an obligation to them. It wasn't any conscious thing on my part. It just seemed like every year there were fewer fish."

Tom Jay is a widely respected sculptor, poet and salmon activist who has lived on the Olympic Peninsula for more than 30 years. One of the founders, with his wife, Mall Johani, of Wild Olympic Salmon, Tom has labored tirelessly and successfully to protect and restore salmon, especially chum salmon, in Chimacum and Snow creeks. A large, bearded vigorous man, Tom has gradually and gracefully assumed the mantle of an elder among Jefferson County salmon activists. Several years ago, when the first Olympic Peninsula salmon were added to the growing list of fish protected by the Endanged Species Act, I asked him for his thoughts.

"We have spent the last 150 years spending our neighbors' wealth," Tom said. "We have created our wealth by stealing the wealth of our neighbors, the salmon and the forests."

Tom said that an examination of the root meanings of the words commonly used when discussing salmon is instructive. "Ecology is the 'story of the house,'" he said, "while economics is the 'inventory, the accounting of the estate.'" Tom said that western civilization's habit of placing the health of the economy ahead of the ecosystem has the situation exactly backwards. He said that the 'ecology' is actually the larger entity, and the economy flows from it.

"The listing of salmon is not about us giving up something," he said. "It is about us learning to share. The salmon were willing to feed us for free, but we turned them into money. How stupid was that? Now if we want the salmon to recover, we've got to become neighbors with the salmon and not consumers. Over the last thirty years, we have stopped calling each other neighbors and have begun referring to ourselves as consumers. The word neighbor means 'near fellow dweller,'" he said. "The original meaning of 'consume' was to 'destroy utterly by fire.'"

The words Tom referred to have Greek origins, as do so many words in our culture that reflect complicated ideas, but the first human inhabitants of this rainy land prospered at the same time as the ancient Greeks. The Makah and Quinault, Quiluete and Hoh, Queets and S'Klallam and Ozette created richly textured societies and grappled with how to live an honorable life. They were acute observers of the natural world, accumulating vast stores of the empirical knowledge that we call science today. They also had the grace to know that there are other, equally rich veins of understanding. Their knowledge of the region's steelhead and salmon, its elk and whales and cedar trees was imminently practical, but it was also informed with the broader reach of metaphor and the deeper structure of prayer.

From Washington D.C. to the NMFS offices in Seattle to the managers and politicians in Olympia, the folks in charge of fish and habitat today could not possibly have a more contrary world view. Unfortunately, over the last 150 years, the expressions of that perspective have had the same effect on wild Northwest salmonids that smallpox had on Olympic Peninsula Indian tribes. When many steelhead and salmon stocks were added to the list of endangered species in the 1990s, the responses from these politician and managers were characteristic—a litany of grievances over the requirements of wild salmonids, rather than grief over what they had done to them. The long-term prospects of West End steelhead, as a result, seem murky at best.

"The front line managers need to lead the way," Jim Lichatowich told me on a rainy fall afternoon in the upper

Dungeness Valley. "But all their measures now are industrial measures, all reflect the values of an industrial economy. Harvest and hatcheries must be reformed so the emphasis is on natural production in rivers. If the front line agencies cannot reform in the face of the ESA, you can't expect other people to.

"What were they going to do?" he asked with a rueful expression. "Let them go extinct?"

I'm pretty much an unreconstructed Celtic heathen, but at this point prayer for these fish seems like as good an idea as anything.